All About Worms

by The Bug Collective

All About Worms

©2024, The Bug Collective. All rights reserved.

No part of this publication may be reproduced, distributed, or transmitted in any form or by any means, including photocopying, recording, or other electronic or mechanical methods, without the prior written permission of the publisher, except in the case of brief quotations embodied in critical reviews and certain other noncommercial uses permitted by copyright law. For permission requests, write to the publisher at the address below.

Edelweiss Creations
Edelweisscreationsllc@gmail.com
ISBN: 9798879485066

First Edition

All About Worms

Contents

1. Introduction to Worms — 5
2. The World of Worms — 9
3. Anatomy of a Worm — 15
4. The Life Cycle of a Worm — 21
5. Classification of a Worm — 25
6. Worm Habitats — 31
7. Worm Behavior — 37
8. The Benefits of Worms — 41
9. Worms and the Environment — 45
10. Worms and Human History — 51
11. Worms in Pop Culture — 57
12. Worms in Science Fiction — 63
13. Worms in Digital Realms — 69
14. Fun Facts about Worms — 75
15. Glossary — 79

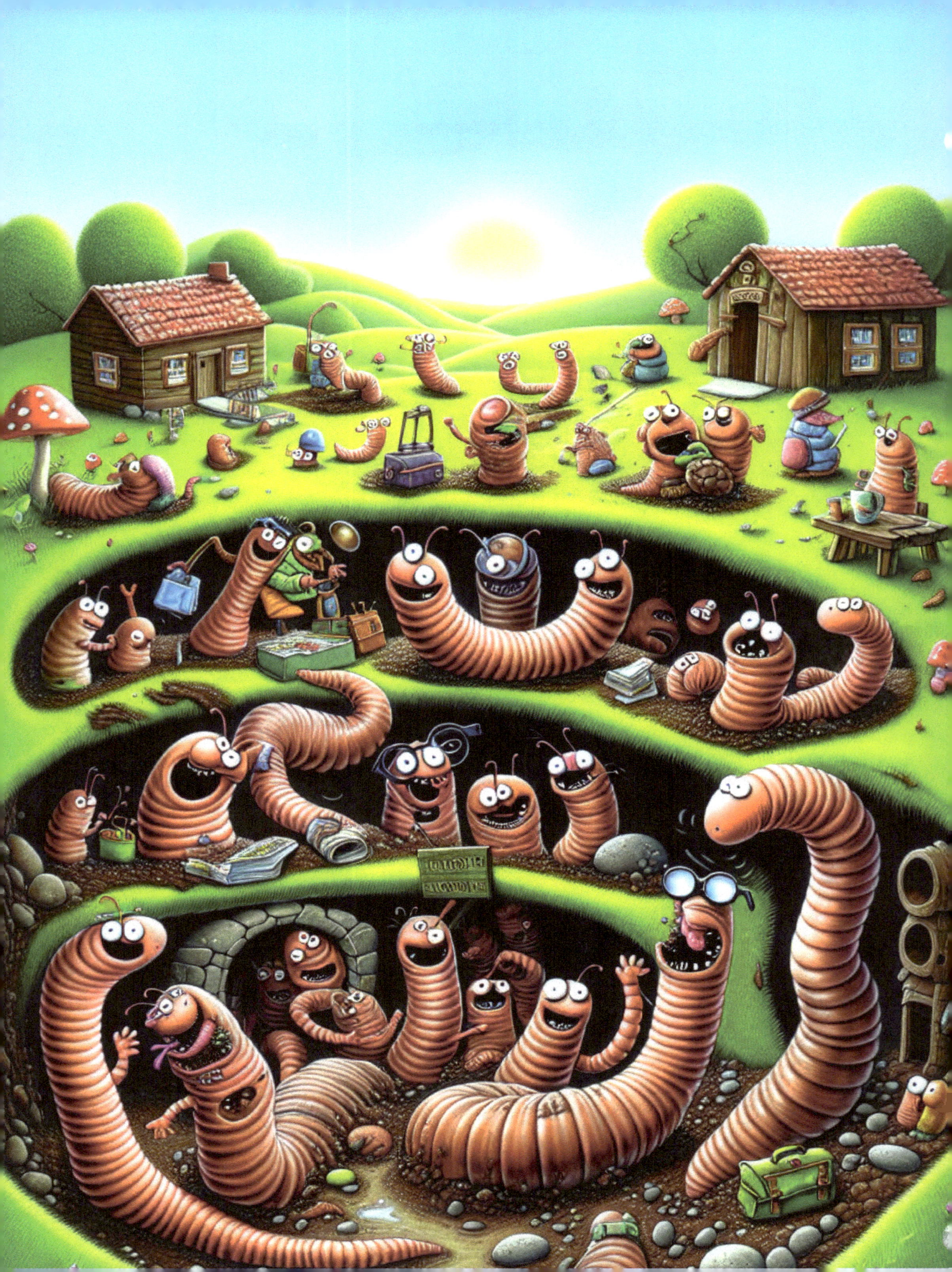

All About Worms

Introduction to Worms

Welcome to the fascinating world of worms! These little creatures may seem unassuming at first glance, but they play a vital role in our ecosystem. In this chapter, we will delve into the intricate world of worms, exploring their anatomy, behavior, and the essential role they play in our environment.

Worms, also known as annelids, are segmented invertebrates that belong to the phylum Annelida. They come in various shapes and sizes, from the delightful thread-like nematodes to the majestic earthworms that can measure up to several meters in length. Now, before we dive deep into the world of worms, let's address the elephant in the room – or should I say, the worm in the room. No, not the bookworm devouring literature, but the humble worm that can make anyone squirm or giggle in equal parts.

While some may view worms as slimy and "gross," they possess a wealth of intriguing characteristics. But fear not, for once you understand their incredible capabilities and the role they play in our ecosystem, you might just fnd yourself developing a newfound appreciation for these squiggly creatures. So, let's set aside any preconceived notions and embark on this wiggly adventure of discovery!

To start our exploration, let's focus on worms' anatomy. These enigmatic creatures are composed of numerous segments, each housing vital organs and muscles. Just like a train made up of individual carriages, their body is divided into compartments, giving worms the flexibility and versatility to maneuver through various environments. It's like they're performing their own earthworm aerobics routine, all while digging through the soil and providing an excellent workout for their muscles!

Did you know that worms don't have lungs? Instead, they rely on their moist skin to breathe. To ensure they receive enough oxygen, they carry out a unique process called cutaneous respiration. This means they absorb oxygen directly through their skin and release carbon dioxide into the environment. It's like they're constantly having a spa day, with their skin rejuvenating and detoxifying as they breathe in the fresh air!

Now, let's talk about behavior. Worms have a knack for burrowing, and boy, are they good at it! Armed with their specialized muscles and slimy secretions, they can navigate through the ground with ease. They create intricate tunnel systems as they munch on organic matter, processing and digesting it into rich, nutrient- packed castings. It's like they're the underground architects, constructing intricate networks while enjoying a tasty soil buffet.

In fact, worms are the ultimate recyclers of the soil. By breaking down organic matter like fallen leaves, dead plant material, and even animal waste, they help to enrich the soil with valuable nutrients. They're like the compost kings and queens, turning nature's leftovers into nutritious feasts for plants to thrive on.

But worms aren't just expert diggers and architects. They also possess an uncanny ability to regenerate. If a worm happens to lose a segment due to a hungry predator or an unfortunate accident, fear not! They can regrow that segment and continue their journey as if nothing happened. It's like having a secret superhero power hidden beneath their soft, unassuming exterior.

Now, let's address the topic of reproduction. Without it, none of us would be here, right? Well, worms have their unique ways of ensuring their species' survival. Some worms reproduce by laying eggs, while others engage in a peculiar process called hermaphroditism. Yes, you heard it right! They have both male and female reproductive organs.

Speaking of reproduction, did you know that certain species of worms are capable of asexual reproduction? That means they can clone themselves! Imagine if humans could do that; the world might be filled with countless copies of the same person. It would certainly make family gatherings interesting!

As we dive deeper into the world of worms, we'll explore the diverse classifications of these fascinating creatures. From the free-living nematodes in the soil to the aquatic polychaetes with their vibrant colors, each group presents its own wonders and quirks. It's like a fabulous worm costume party, with each attendee showcasing their unique traits.

Throughout this book, we will uncover the intricate details of worms, from their feeding habits and habitats to their interactions with other organisms. We will explore the symbiotic relationships they form with plants and the crucial role they play in recycling organic matter. So, get ready to venture into the captivating underground realm of worms. But let me warn you, once you start unraveling the secrets of these remarkable creatures, you may fnd yourself wormed into their world forever!

Now, let's dig in and begin our journey into the captivating realm of worms! Remember, even the smallest and most humble organisms can hold astonishing truths and bring a smile to your face, even if it's a subtle worm joke. So, brace yourself for a delightful adventure that will leave you in awe of these squirming wonders beneath our feet.

Let's embark on this fascinating wormly expedition together!

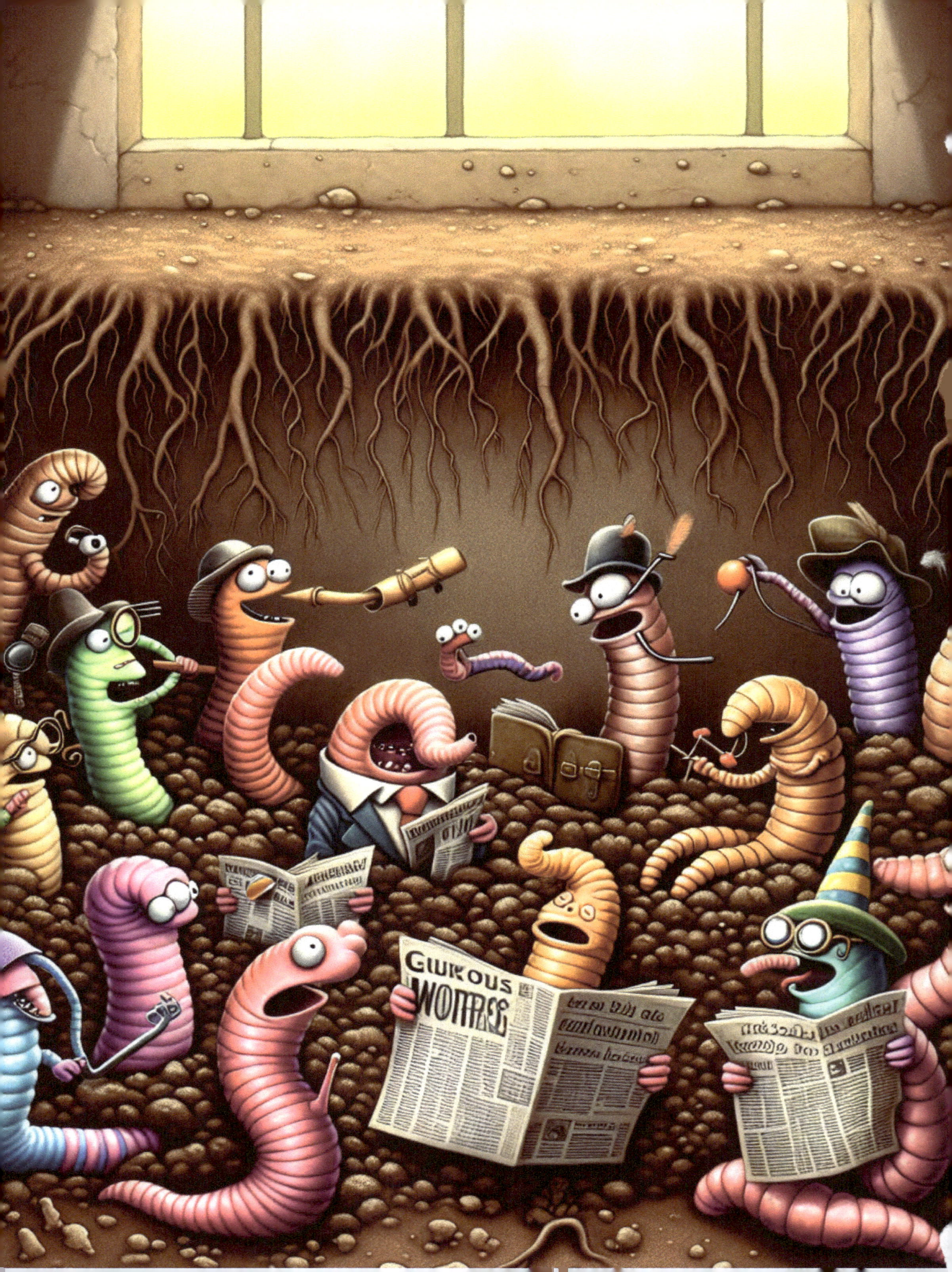

All About Worms

The World of Worms

In a world beneath our feet, there exists a hidden kingdom teeming with life. This is the world of worms, a fascinating realm that often goes unnoticed by the human eye. In this chapter, we will embark on a journey to explore the intricacies and wonders of this subterranean universe.

As we descend into the depths of the soil, transported by our imagination, we fnd ourselves in a place where darkness reigns but life thrives. The soil trembles with the movement of countless tiny bodies, brushing against one another in a complex dance of survival and cooperation.

Our journey leads us to a bustling metropolis of worms, where diverse species coexist in harmony. The great Earth King, a majestic earthworm, presides over the kingdom, his massive presence a testament to the wisdom and strength of his kind. As we approach, he graciously welcomes us, conveying a sense of ancient wisdom accumulated over generations.

"Welcome," he says in a deep, rumbling voice, "to the heart of our kingdom. Here, life pulses in every inch of soil, offering sustenance, shelter, and a sense of purpose to all who reside within."

And so, we immerse ourselves in this hidden world, observing the intricate workings of the worms. Each species in this underground realm has perfected its own unique skillset to contribute to the circle of life.

The diligent soil engineers, known as burrowers, tirelessly dig intricate tunnels that serve as highways and homes for their community.

These tunnels, like the veins of the earth, connect distant corners of the kingdom, allowing worms to roam freely and exchange resources. As we wander along the dark tunnels, we witness the astonishing architectural prowess of the burrowers. They create chambers lined with organic material, meticulously fashioned pathways that guide rainwater downwards to prevent flooding, and intricate networks of underground highways.

Among the burrowers, we encounter the architectural artists, a specialized group of worms with an innate ability to construct elaborate chambers and galleries that serve different purposes. Some chambers serve as nurseries for their young, carefully constructed with enough space to accommodate growing families. Others act as storage rooms, where gatherers bring their bounties of organic matter to be stored for times of scarcity within the kingdom.

As we observe their diligent work, we are struck by the immense thought and effort put into their creations. Each chamber and tunnel is carefully constructed, ensuring stability and functionality. The burrowers possess an innate sense of geology, understanding the composition of the soil and how it can support the structures they build.

Moving deeper into the kingdom, we encounter the composters, the masters of decomposition, who play an indispensable role in the circle of life. These worms feast on decaying matter, breaking it down into fine particles, enriching the soil with nutrients. Their efforts set in motion a never-ending cycle of transformation, where waste becomes nourishment, and death gives birth to new life.

We witness their intricate feeding process, as they consume everything from leaf litter to fallen trees. Their powerful digestive systems, equipped with enzymes and microbes, break down complex compounds into simpler forms, creating a fertile stew of organic matter.

From above, we hear the melodic hum of millions of microorganisms, busily transforming these organic morsels into nourishment that will sustain the kingdom's plants. With every bite they take, the composters unleash a symphony of microbial activity, breaking down complex molecules and liberating vital nutrients.

And as these decomposers toil relentlessly, so too do the gatherers, the swift worms who have honed the skill of locating and hoarding valuable organic matter. They leave no stone unturned, no leaf disregarded, as they tirelessly collect morsels of sustenance to store within the depths of their burrows, ensuring their survival during lean times.

With awe, we observe their foraging techniques. Some gatherers comb through the leaf litter on the forest floor, detecting hidden caches of decaying matter and swiftly transporting them back to their burrows. Others venture into the depths of compost heaps, where the organic feast is plentiful. They work with exceptional speed, scavenging every resource they can find, in a constant race against time and competitors.

As we wander deeper within this underground realm, the darkness intensifies, and the soil feels more alive than ever. We encounter the recyclers, worms with a fondness for fine dining. These voracious creatures, known as detritivores, devour a wide range of debris, from decaying vegetation to animal waste. Their insatiable appetites transform what would be seen as refuse by many into vital nutrients that nourish plants and sustain the delicate balance of the ecosystem.

In their quest for sustenance, we witness their astonishing ability to consume and process large volumes of organic matter. Their digestive systems, equipped with specialized enzymes and microbes, break down complex molecules into simpler forms, converting them into bioavailable nutrients that can promote growth and vitality within the soil.

But it is not only through their dietary habits that worms contribute to the grand tapestry of life. Throughout the kingdom, worms engage in intimate symbiotic relationships, forming alliances that benefit all parties involved. In their tunnels, they host microscopic communities of bacteria and fungi, working together to break down complex organic compounds and unlock their hidden energy. These partnerships not only fuel the growth of plants but also serve as a testament to the interconnectedness and interdependence of all living beings.

As our expedition comes to an end, we are left in awe of the hidden marvels that dwell beneath our feet. The world of worms is a constant reminder that even in the darkest depths, life flourishes and intricate ecosystems thrive. Their tireless efforts to nurture and sustain the soil highlight the vital role they play in maintaining the delicate balance of nature.

And so, as we bid farewell to the Earth King and his noble subjects, we ascend back to the surface, filled with a newfound appreciation for the humble worm. We walk upon the earth, knowing that beneath our every step lies a miniature kingdom, silently contributing to the richness and diversity of life. Let us remember the world of worms and honor their essential role in the tapestry of existence.

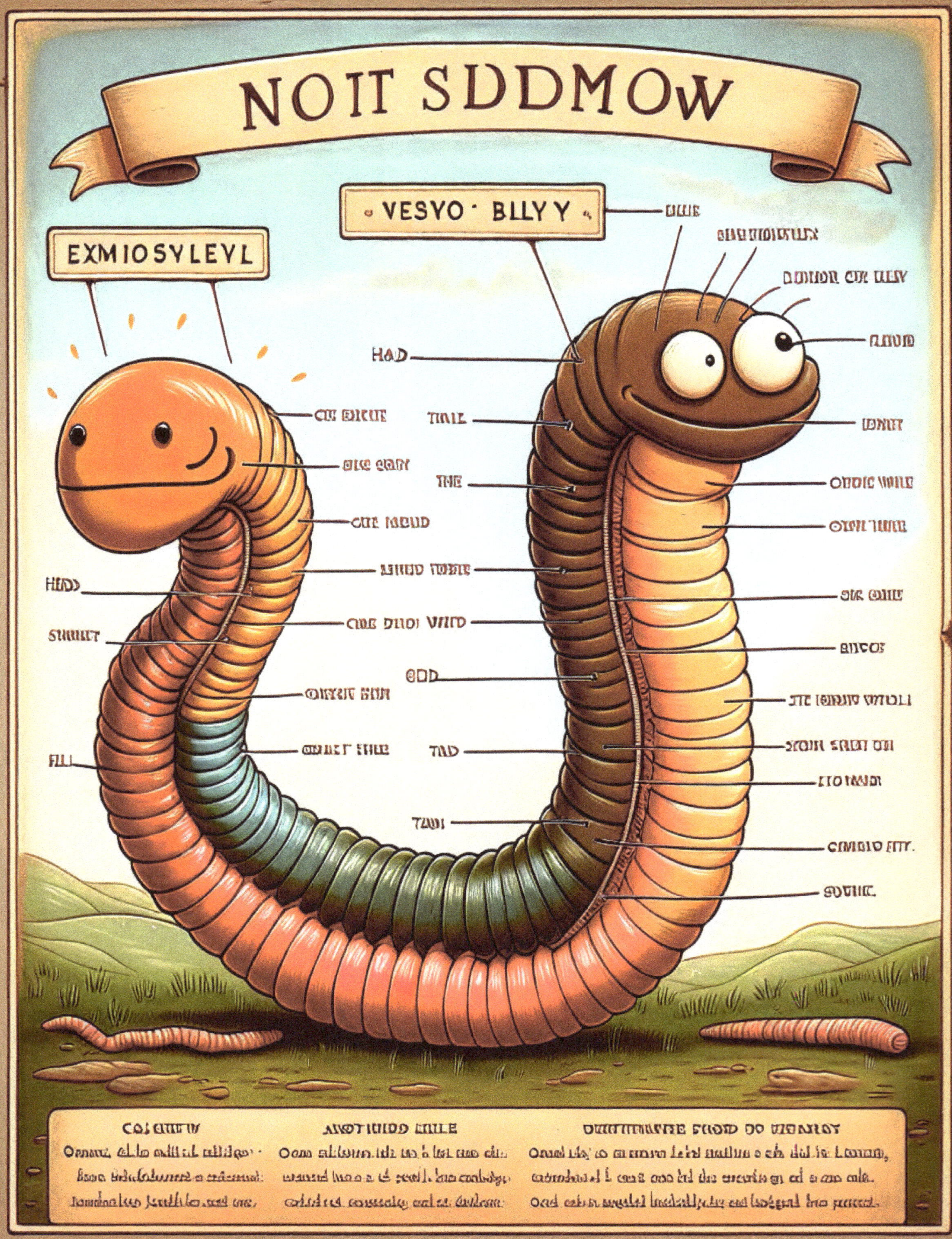
NOIT SDDMOW
VESYO · BLLY Y
EXMIOSYLEVL
HAD
TNE
TAD

Anatomy of a Worm

Worms may appear simple at first glance, but their anatomy is quite fascinating. Although they lack complex structures like vertebrates, they are finely adapted to their underground lifestyle. Let's explore the anatomy of a worm in detail.

The External Features:

Worms typically have a long, cylindrical body that is divided into several segments called metameres. Each segment contains specific organs and structures crucial for their survival. The outermost layer of their body is known as the epidermis, which secretes mucus to aid in movement through the soil. The mucus not only reduces friction but also helps to prevent desiccation or drying out.

At the anterior end of the worm is the prostomium, which acts as the sensory organ and helps in navigation. It has specialized receptors that allow the worm to sense changes in temperature, humidity, light, and chemicals in the environment. The prostomium also plays a role in collecting and filtering the food particles from the soil.

Worms may possess sensory bristles called setae that protrude from their body wall. The number and arrangement of setae vary depending on the species. These setae assist in gripping the soil while burrowing, as well as providing tactile information, enabling the worm to detect vibrations and changes in its surroundings.

The Digestive System:

Worms have a relatively simple, yet efficient digestive system. They take in food through their mouth, which is located on the first segment. From there, the food travels through the pharynx, a muscular tube that helps draw in and grind the food particles. The pharynx leads to the esophagus, which connects to the crop, where food storage occurs.

After leaving the crop, the food moves into the gizzard, which contains tiny stones and gritty particles for grinding up the ingested soil and organic matter. The gizzard's powerful muscles contract and relax, churning the food and breaking it down further. This grinding process, combined with the abrasiveness of the stones, helps the worm extract as many nutrients as possible from its diet.

From the gizzard, the partially broken down food enters the intestine, a long and coiled tube to maximize nutrient absorption. The intestine is lined with microscopic finger-like projections called villi, which increase the surface area for absorption.

Nutrients are absorbed into the worm's body, while undigested waste, called castings, are eliminated through the anus.

The Circulatory System:

Worms have a unique circulatory system called the closed circulatory system. This system consists of blood vessels that carry a specialized fluid called hemolymph.

The hemolymph functions as both blood and lymph, carrying nutrients and oxygen to the various tissues and organs of the worm.

The circulatory system of a worm consists of a dorsal blood vessel that runs on top of the pharynx, along with five smaller ventral blood vessels that lie parallel to the nerve cord underneath the digestive system. These blood vessels distribute the hemolymph efficiently throughout the worm's body, ensuring the transport of nutrients and waste products.

The circulatory system also helps in regulating the worm's body temperature. As worms are cold-blooded organisms, the distribution of hemolymph can aid in heat exchange with the environment, helping to maintain optimal body temperature for their survival.

The Respiratory System:

In place of lungs, worms possess a respiratory system that allows for gas exchange through their moist skin. Oxygen from the surrounding environment can diffuse through their skin and enter into the bloodstream. Carbon dioxide, a waste product, is also expelled through the skin.

Worms rely on a thin, moist cuticle that covers their body as a barrier between their internal organs and the external environment. This cuticle helps maintain moisture, which is essential for efficient respiration. The thinness of their body allows for a rapid exchange of gasses, ensuring a constant supply of oxygen and the removal of carbon dioxide.

The cuticle not only aids in respiration but also provides protection against predators and abrasions during burrowing. It acts as a flexible armor, preventing injury and allowing the worm to navigate through the soil with ease.

The Nervous System:

While worms lack a centralized brain, they possess a distinct nervous system that allows for coordinated movement and sensory functions. The nervous system of a worm consists of a pair of ganglia (clusters of nerve cells) in each segment of their body, connected by a ventral nerve cord.

These ganglia act as local command centers, coordinating the actions of each segment. The ventral nerve cord relays information between these ganglia, ensuring smooth and coherent motion. Sensory cells positioned throughout the worm's body detect various stimuli, such as touch, vibrations, or chemical signals, and transmit these signals to the ganglia for processing.

The nervous system of worms enables them to respond to changes in their environment, guiding their burrowing, feeding, and mating behaviors. Despite having a decentralized nervous system, worms can exhibit complex behaviors and even learn from their experiences. Studies have shown that worms can learn to associate certain stimuli with rewards or punishments, demonstrating a level of cognitive ability previously unrecognized in these humble creatures.

The Reproductive System:

Worms are hermaphroditic, each possessing both male and female reproductive organs. This reproductive strategy enables self-fertilization. During mating, two worms align their bodies to exchange sperm through an opening called the genital pore, located on the ventral side of their body.

The exchanged sperm is stored in specialized structures called seminal receptacles within each worm. When ready to lay eggs, each worm produces a mucus cocoon that contains a small number of fertilized eggs. The cocoon, produced in the clitellum region of their body, slips over the worm's head and travels backward before being filled with eggs and sperm.

The cocoon then slips off the worm's body and is deposited into the soil. Within a few weeks, the cocoon hatches, releasing tiny worms, which then begin their journey in the soil. This unique reproductive strategy ensures genetic variation within the population and ensures the survival of the species.

Remarkably, worms can also exhibit asexual reproduction under certain conditions. If environmental conditions become unfavorable or resources are scarce, some species of worms can reproduce through a process called parthenogenesis, where new individuals are generated from unfertilized eggs. This ability allows worms to adapt to changing environments and rapidly increase their population size when needed.

The amazing ability of worms to regenerate their body is another noteworthy aspect. If a worm is injured or severed, it has the remarkable capability to regenerate its lost segments and continue living. This regenerative power has fascinated scientists for years and has opened avenues of research in the feld of regenerative medicine.

Understanding the intricate anatomy of a worm provides insight into their unique adaptations and survival strategies. By delving into the fascinating world beneath the surface, we gain a deeper appreciation for these remarkable creatures and their pivotal role in the ecosystem.

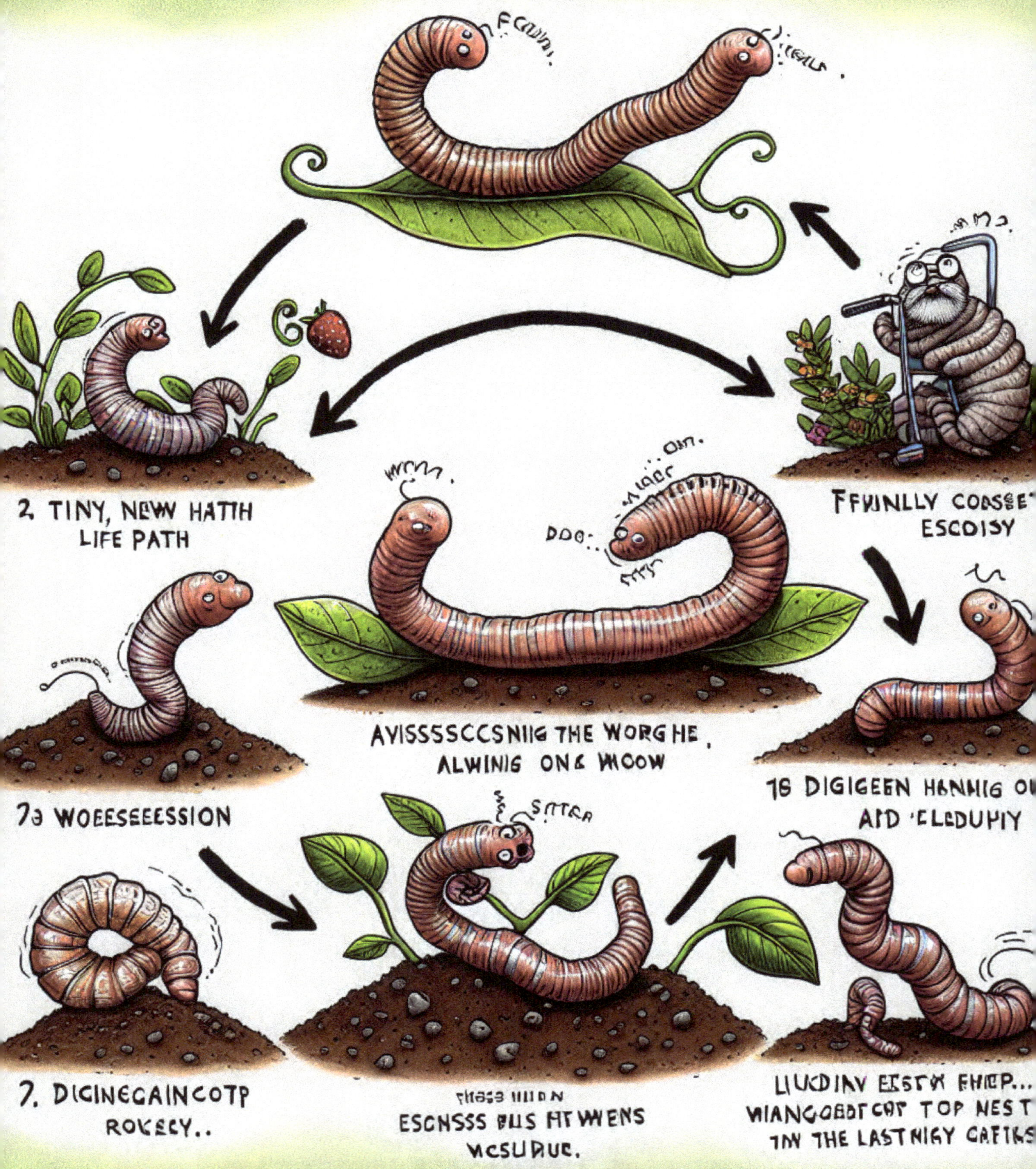
2. TINY, NEW HATTH
LIFE PATH
FFWNLLY COBSSE
ESCOISY
AVISSSSCCSNIG THE WORG HE,
ALWINIG ONG MOOW
7ə WOEESEEESSION
16 DIGIGEEN HENNIG O
AID 'ELEDUPIY
7. DICINEGAINCOTP
ROKECY..
ESCNSSS BUS HTWENS
MCSURUC.
LIUCDIAV EESTY EHEP...
WIANGOBDT COT TOP NEST
THY THE LASTNIGY CAFIKS

The Life Cycle of a Worm

Worms undergo a fascinating and complex life cycle that involves several stages of development. By delving deeper into the intricacies of their growth and reproduction, we can gain a greater understanding of these remarkable creatures.

The life cycle of a worm begins with the laying of eggs. Worm eggs are designed to withstand challenging conditions, ensuring the survival of the species. The eggs are typically small and may be encased in a protective shell or cocoon. This outer layer shields them from extreme temperatures, predators, and unfavorable environmental conditions. The size and appearance of worm eggs can differ among species. Some are barely visible to the naked eye, while others are larger and more distinct. It is fascinating to observe how worms meticulously select suitable spots to deposit their eggs, such as moist soil, decaying vegetation, or even inside the bodies of other organisms. This diversity in egg-laying sites reflects the adaptability of worms to various environments.

After a certain period, the eggs hatch, marking the transition into the next stage of the worm's life cycle. Tiny hatchlings, often referred to as juveniles, emerge from the eggs. At this point, these young worms are delicate and lack some of the distinct characteristics of their adult counterparts. They rely heavily on their environment for sustenance and protection, seeking out suitable food sources and hiding places to ensure their survival. The rate of hatching can be influenced by temperature, moisture levels, and other environmental factors. Some species have specific requirements for hatching, while others are more adaptable, allowing them to thrive in a wide range of conditions.

As the juveniles grow, they undergo a gradual metamorphosis. This process involves the development of the physical features and traits that defne adult worms. Their bodies undergo elongation, and segments become more pronounced, acquiring the unique characteristics of their species. During this critical stage, the worms mature both physically and behaviorally, acquiring the skills and instincts that allow them to thrive in their environment. They learn to navigate their surroundings, avoid predators, and seek out suitable food sources. Growth rates at this stage can vary, influenced by factors such as food availability and environmental conditions. Some species reach maturity quickly, while others take longer to develop.

Once a worm reaches maturity, which varies depending on the species and environmental conditions, it becomes capable of reproduction. Worms have remarkable reproductive mechanisms that contribute to their success as a species. Some species reproduce asexually, meaning they can regenerate their bodies from a severed part, enabling them to colonize new areas quickly. This process, known as fragmentation, allows worms to multiply rapidly and exploit favorable environments. Other species engage in sexual reproduction, where worms exchange sperm to fertilize eggs internally. This diversity in reproductive strategies highlights the adaptability of worms and their ability to ensure the survival of their lineage. The timing of reproduction can be influenced by seasonal changes, availability of mates, and environmental cues, ensuring that offspring have the best chance of survival.

At the mature stage, worms begin actively producing eggs. The rate and quantity of egg production can vary significantly among species. Certain worms lay a few eggs sporadically, while others produce hundreds or

Classification of a Worm

Worms are a fascinating group of organisms that exhibit incredible diversity in their characteristics and features. To better understand and study worms, scientists have classified them into different groups based on various criteria. In this chapter, we will explore the classification of worms and delve deeper into the three major phyla they belong to: Annelida, Nematoda, and Platyhelminthes.

The phylum Annelida includes segmented worms, which are characterized by their body divided into distinct segments. Annelids are among the most diverse and numerous invertebrates on Earth, with over 22,000 described species. They can be found in a myriad of environments, ranging from marine and freshwater habitats to terrestrial ecosystems. Examples of annelids include earthworms, leeches, and marine worms.

Annelids possess a closed circulatory system, meaning that they have blood vessels that transport blood throughout their bodies. This type of circulatory system allows for efficient oxygen transport and waste removal. The segments of annelids often house various specialized structures, such as setae, bristles that aid in locomotion, and parapodia, fleshy outgrowths that function as gills in some marine species. Additionally, annelids exhibit a well-developed nervous system, with a chain of ganglia (nerve clusters) running along their ventral side.

Earthworms, belonging to the class Clitellata within Annelida, are one of the most well-known annelids. They play a crucial role in soil health and ecosystem functioning. Earthworms are remarkable organisms that contribute to nutrient cycling by consuming organic matter such as leaves and decomposing it, thereby releasing nutrients that can be utilized by plants. Their burrowing activities also improve soil structure, drainage, and aeration. This aerobic environment is essential for the survival of beneficial soil microorganisms and plant roots.

Apart from earthworms, another notable group within the phylum Annelida is the polychaetes. Polychaetes are primarily marine worms that display incredible diversity in their forms and lifestyles. They can be found in various marine habitats, including coral reefs, intertidal zones, and deep-sea environments. Polychaetes exhibit a wide range of feeding strategies, such as filter feeding, scavenging, predation, and even parasitism. Some species construct intricate tubes or burrows in the sediment, creating microhabitats for other organisms and influencing the overall structure of marine ecosystems.

The phylum Nematoda comprises roundworms, which are slender and unsegmented worms. These creatures are astonishingly diverse, with estimates of up to 500,000 species worldwide, although only a fraction have been described so far. Nematodes occupy nearly every habitat on Earth, from the oceans' deepest trenches to the soil beneath our feet. They can also be found in plants, animals, and even humans, often acting as parasites.

The ecological roles of nematodes are diverse and complex. In soil ecosystems, nematodes play crucial roles in nutrient cycling, decomposition, and regulation of plant populations. Some nematodes are beneficial to plant health, while others are harmful pests causing diseases in crops. Nematodes also serve as indicators of soil quality and ecosystem health, as shifts in nematode communities can reflect disturbances or changes in land use practices. Furthermore, several even thousands in a short timeframe. The reproductive capacity of worms is influenced by factors such as food availability, age, and environmental conditions. By depositing eggs in their environment, worms guarantee the continuity of their species, contributing to the overall balance and diversity of ecosystems. These eggs can be dispersed through various means, including wind, water, or the transport by other organisms. Such dispersal mechanisms ensure that worms have the opportunity to colonize new areas and thrive in different habitats.

Like all living beings, worms have a limited lifespan. The factors influencing the lifespan of worms are multifaceted and can include environmental conditions, availability of food, predation, and genetic factors. As worms age, they may experience a decline in their physiological functions, becoming less efficient at foraging and reproducing. Once they reach the end of their life cycle, worms provide an essential ecological service as they decompose and return valuable nutrients back to the soil, enriching it for future generations of organisms. The decomposition of worms contributes to the overall health of ecosystems, fostering nutrient cycling and maintaining the balance of organic matter in the soil.

Understanding the intricate life cycle of worms provides a comprehensive view of their vital role in nature. It unveils the processes that contribute to the persistence and diversity of worm populations, influencing soil health, nutrient cycling, and overall ecosystem dynamics. By unraveling the secrets of these seemingly simple creatures, we gain a deeper appreciation for the incredible complexity and interconnectedness of life on Earth. The study of worms and their life cycles continues to captivate researchers, revealing new insights into the mechanisms that enable these organisms to thrive and contribute to the rich tapestry of life.

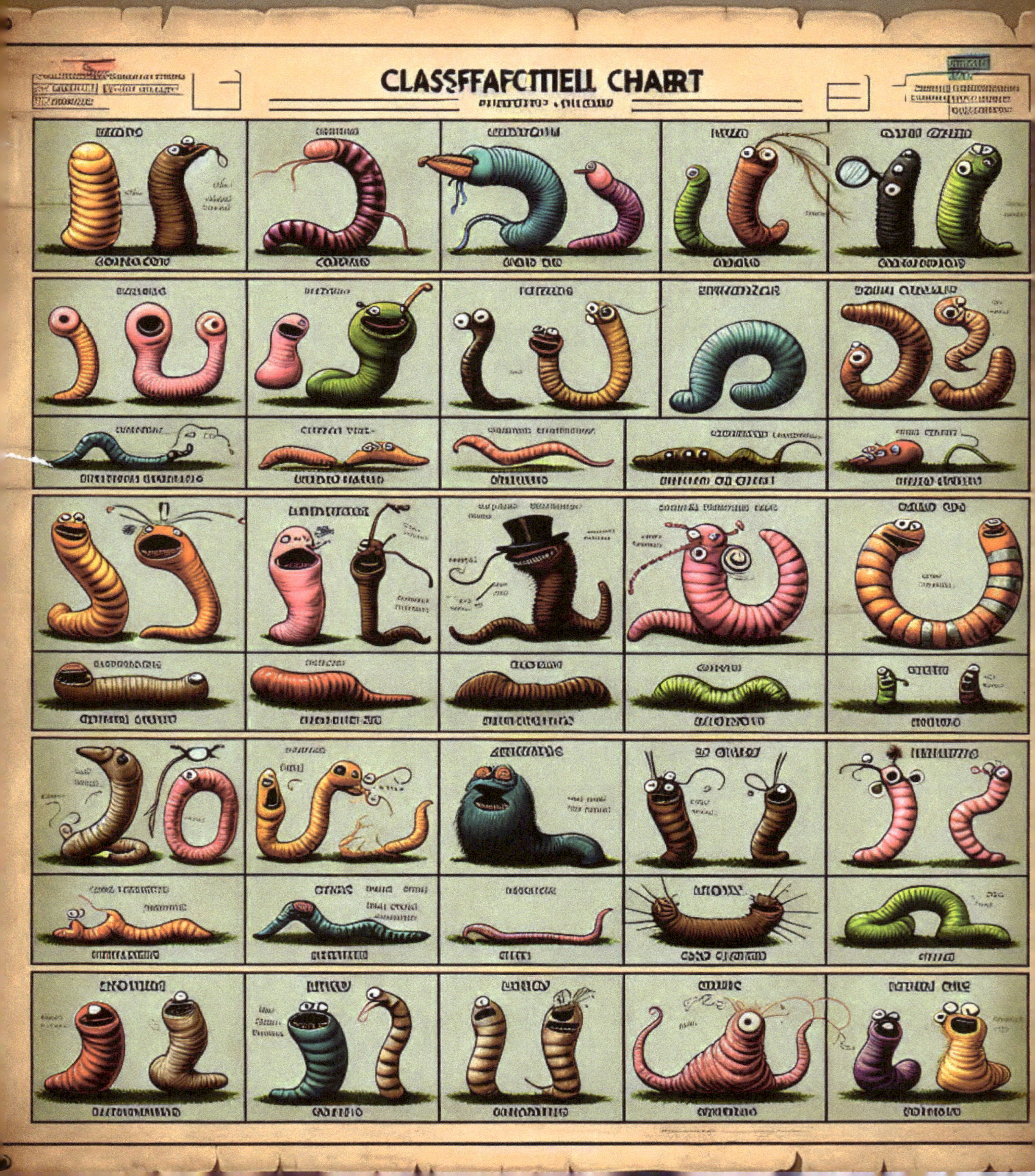
CLASSFFAFCITIELL CHART

Classification of a Worm

Worms are a fascinating group of organisms that exhibit incredible diversity in their characteristics and features. To better understand and study worms, scientists have classified them into different groups based on various criteria. In this chapter, we will explore the classification of worms and delve deeper into the three major phyla they belong to: Annelida, Nematoda, and Platyhelminthes.

The phylum Annelida includes segmented worms, which are characterized by their body divided into distinct segments. Annelids are among the most diverse and numerous invertebrates on Earth, with over 22,000 described species. They can be found in a myriad of environments, ranging from marine and freshwater habitats to terrestrial ecosystems. Examples of annelids include earthworms, leeches, and marine worms.

Annelids possess a closed circulatory system, meaning that they have blood vessels that transport blood throughout their bodies. This type of circulatory system allows for efficient oxygen transport and waste removal. The segments of annelids often house various specialized structures, such as setae, bristles that aid in locomotion, and parapodia, fleshy outgrowths that function as gills in some marine species. Additionally, annelids exhibit a well-developed nervous system, with a chain of ganglia (nerve clusters) running along their ventral side.

Earthworms, belonging to the class Clitellata within Annelida, are one of the most well-known annelids. They play a crucial role in soil health and ecosystem functioning. Earthworms are remarkable organisms that contribute to nutrient cycling by consuming organic matter such as leaves and decomposing it, thereby releasing nutrients that can be utilized by plants. Their burrowing activities also improve soil structure, drainage, and aeration. This aerobic environment is essential for the survival of beneficial soil microorganisms and plant roots.

Apart from earthworms, another notable group within the phylum Annelida is the polychaetes. Polychaetes are primarily marine worms that display incredible diversity in their forms and lifestyles. They can be found in various marine habitats, including coral reefs, intertidal zones, and deep-sea environments. Polychaetes exhibit a wide range of feeding strategies, such as filter feeding, scavenging, predation, and even parasitism. Some species construct intricate tubes or burrows in the sediment, creating microhabitats for other organisms and influencing the overall structure of marine ecosystems.

The phylum Nematoda comprises roundworms, which are slender and unsegmented worms. These creatures are astonishingly diverse, with estimates of up to 500,000 species worldwide, although only a fraction have been described so far. Nematodes occupy nearly every habitat on Earth, from the oceans' deepest trenches to the soil beneath our feet. They can also be found in plants, animals, and even humans, often acting as parasites.

The ecological roles of nematodes are diverse and complex. In soil ecosystems, nematodes play crucial roles in nutrient cycling, decomposition, and regulation of plant populations. Some nematodes are beneficial to plant health, while others are harmful pests causing diseases in crops. Nematodes also serve as indicators of soil quality and ecosystem health, as shifts in nematode communities can reflect disturbances or changes in land use practices. Furthermore, several nematode species have been studied extensively for their potential as biological control agents for pests, promoting sustainable agriculture.

Nematodes possess a unique body structure that allows them to occupy various habitats. They have a tough cuticle that protects their delicate bodies and aids in resistance against environmental challenges. Some nematodes have specialized adaptations, such as the ability to survive extreme temperatures, high pressures, and desiccation. Additionally, their reproductive strategies can be diverse, including sexual and asexual reproduction, with some species capable of producing an incredible number of offspring.

The phylum Platyhelminthes includes flatworms, which have a flattened body shape. Flatworms can be found in a wide array of environments, including freshwater, marine, and terrestrial habitats. They can be classified into three major groups: free-living flatworms, flukes, and tapeworms. Examples of free-living flatworms are planarians, which are often utilized in regenerative studies due to their remarkable regenerative abilities.

Flatworms differ from annelids and nematodes in terms of body organization. They lack specialized respiratory and circulatory systems, relying on diffusion to exchange gases and nutrients with their surroundings. Their nervous system is relatively simple compared to that of annelids but is still capable of coordinating their movements and behaviors. Flatworms exhibit an extraordinary capacity for regeneration, with some species capable of regenerating an entire individual from just a tiny piece of tissue.

The diverse group of free-living flatworms includes species that vary in size, habitat preferences, and feeding strategies. Some flatworms are predators, preying on small invertebrates, while others may scavenge or filter feed. Many free-living flatworms possess photoreceptor cells and even simple eyespots, which allow them to detect and respond to light stimuli. These adaptations aid in finding food, avoiding predators, and navigating their environments.

Flukes and tapeworms are parasitic flatworms, which have complex life cycles involving multiple host species. They have specialized adaptations to thrive in their parasitic lifestyle. For example, flukes often have complex reproductive systems, producing large numbers of eggs that are released into the environment through the host's feces. These eggs then infect intermediate hosts, such as snails, where they develop further before being released into another host, such as a mammal or bird. Tapeworms, on the other hand, possess a series of reproductive segments called proglottids, which release fertilized eggs into the host's digestive system.

The classification of worms provides a framework for understanding the incredible diversity and complexity of these organisms. From the segmented annelids to the round nematodes and the flat flatworms, each group presents unique characteristics and adaptations that have allowed them to thrive in diverse habitats. The ongoing research in this feld, fueled by molecular biology and genetic sequencing techniques, continues to unveil new insights into the relationships, behaviors, and ecological functions of worms.

Appreciating the significance of worms goes beyond their scientific study. Worms, in their various forms, play vital roles in ecosystems, contributing to nutrient cycling, soil health, and decomposition. Furthermore, their interactions with other organisms, such as plants, animals, and humans, can have profound implications for our well-being. Understanding and conserving these often overlooked and underestimated creatures is crucial for maintaining the delicate balance of our planet's ecosystem

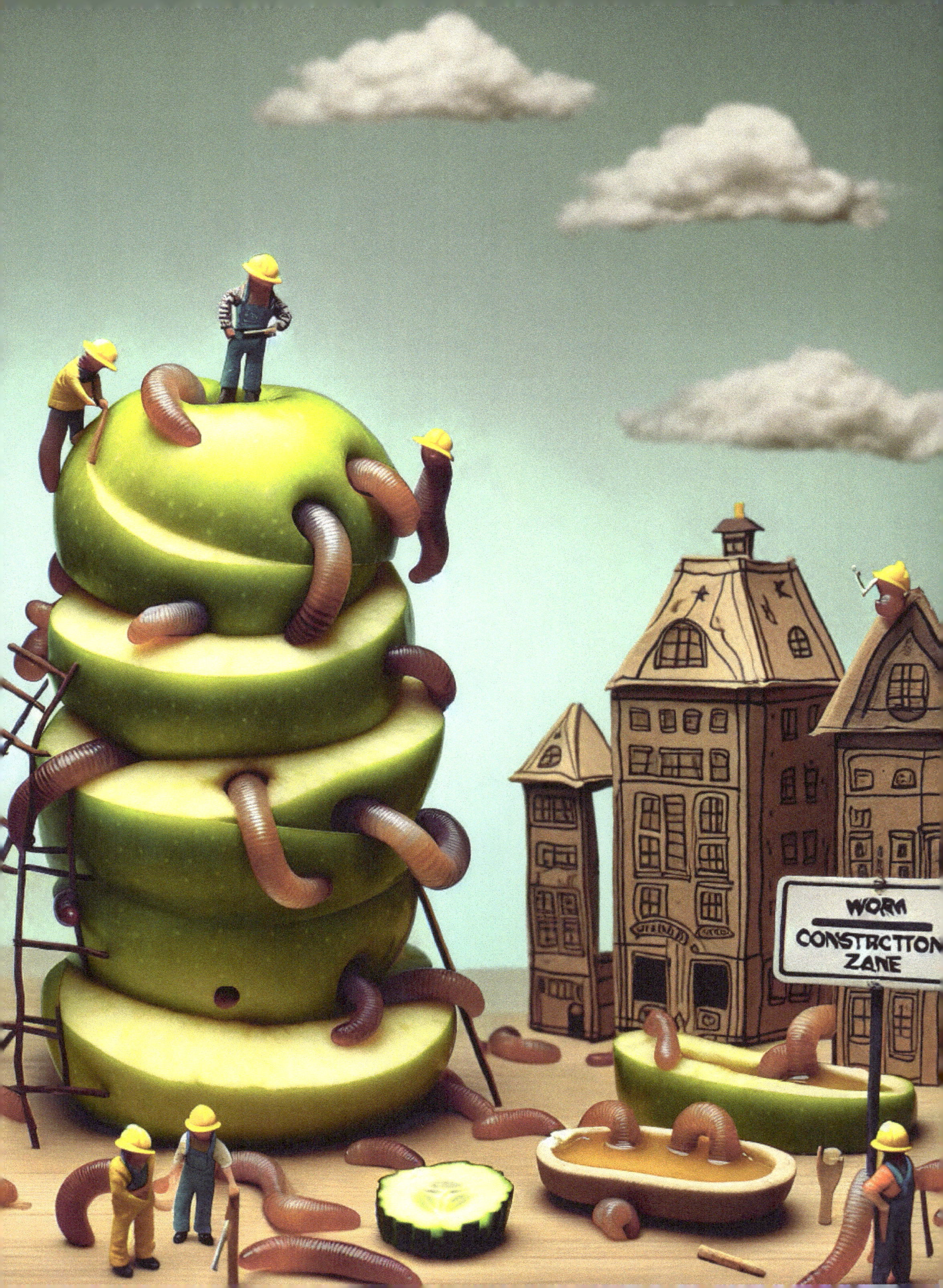
WORM
CONSTRCTTON
ZANE

Worm Habitats

Worms can be found in a wide range of habitats, both on land and in water. They are incredibly adaptable creatures and have the ability to thrive in various environments around the world. Let's explore some of the different habitats where worms make their homes.

1. Soil Habitats:

One of the most common habitats for worms is the soil. Earthworms, for example, are found in almost every type of soil, from dense forests to open grasslands. They burrow through the soil, creating tunnels and aerating the ground as they move.

This helps to improve soil structure and allows for better water absorption, benefiting plants and other organisms.

There are three main groups of earthworms found in soil habitats: epigeic, endogeic, and anecic. Epigeic earthworms live in the upper layer of the soil, where organic matter like leaf litter accumulates. They are generally small, surface- dwelling worms that feed on decaying plant material. Endogeic earthworms burrow deeper into the soil, creating horizontal burrows. They primarily feed on soil particles and organic matter. Anecic earthworms, on the other hand, create vertical burrows that extend deep into the soil. They bring organic matter from the surface, such as leaves, into their burrows to feed on, and their burrowing activities can greatly improve soil drainage.

2. Freshwater Habitats:

Many species of worms can be found in freshwater ecosystems such as rivers, lakes, and ponds. These worms play a crucial role in maintaining the health of these habitats. They help break down organic matter, recycle nutrients, and provide a food source for other aquatic organisms.

Freshwater worms are adapted to life in aquatic environments. They come in various shapes and sizes, ranging from tiny tube-dwelling worms to larger segmented worms. Some examples include the bloodworm, tubifex worm, and Nais worm. Bloodworms, also known as Chironomidae larvae, are often found in muddy sediments and are known for their bright red color. They are crucial food sources for fsh and aquatic birds. Tubifex worms prefer stagnant water and are often found in polluted environments, feeding on organic waste. They can tolerate low oxygen levels and are commonly used as indicators of poor water quality. The Nais worm is commonly found in clean freshwater habitats and is an important indicator species for water quality. Their presence indicates that the water is clean and unpolluted.

3. Marine Habitats:

Worms are also abundant in marine environments, ranging from shallow coastal waters to the deep sea. Marine worms can be found burrowing in sandy or muddy sediments, hiding in coral reefs, or even thriving in hydrothermal vents. They play important roles in nutrient cycling and contribute to the overall biodiversity of these ecosystems.

Marine worms exhibit incredible diversity, with over 22,000 known species. Some of the most familiar marine worms include the lugworm, sandworm, and feather duster worm. Lugworms, also known as king ragworms, are burrowing worms found in sandy or muddy sediments along coastlines. They create U-shaped burrows and are popular bait for recreational fishing. Their burrowing activities help to oxygenate the sediment and mix organic matter, influencing the overall ecosystem dynamics. Sandworms, similar to lugworms, create burrows in sandy sediments and are also used as bait. They are vital in the energy transfer process as they consume organic matter and are preyed upon by various fish species.

Feather duster worms are filter feeders that construct intricate tube-like structures on rocks or coral reefs. These colorful worms use feathery tentacles to capture plankton from the water for food. They provide a valuable food source for many marine organisms and contribute to the overall biodiversity of coral reef ecosystems.

4. Leaf Litter and Forest Floors:

Worms, such as detritivores, are crucial in leaf litter decomposition and nutrient recycling in forests. They consume fallen leaves and other organic matter, breaking it down into smaller particles that can be further decomposed by fungi and bacteria. This process releases nutrients back into the soil, essential for the growth of plants and trees.

In forest habitats, different species of worms play specific roles in leaf litter decomposition. This includes earthworms, millipedes, and springtails. Earthworms, mostly from the endogeic and anecic groups, feed on leaf litter and help mix organic matter into the soil, enhancing its fertility. By ingesting the decaying plant material, earthworms break it down and release nutrients such as nitrogen and phosphorus into the soil, making them available for plants. Millipedes, with their many legs, consume decaying leaves and plant material, accelerating the decomposition process. They shred the leaves into smaller pieces, increasing the surface area available for microbial decomposition.

Springtails are tiny, wingless insects that feed on organic matter and fungal spores within the leaf litter, aiding in nutrient release. Their feeding habits and excretion contribute to the cycling of carbon and nutrients, facilitating the overall decomposition process.

5. Composting Systems:

Worms, specifically redworms or tiger worms, are often utilized in composting systems. These worms have a voracious appetite for organic waste and are excellent decomposers. They thrive in compost piles, consuming food scraps, yard trimmings, and other organic materials, and producing nutrient-rich castings, known as vermicompost, that can be used as a natural fertilizer.

The use of worms in composting, also known as vermicomposting, has gained significant popularity due to its many benefits. Redworms are commonly used for this purpose because they can consume large amounts of organic waste and have a fast reproductive rate. When organic waste is added to a vermicomposting system, the worms break it down into smaller particles through digestion. The organic matter is partially decomposed through enzymatic action in the worm's gut, resulting in castings that are rich in beneficial microorganisms and nutrients like nitrogen, phosphorus, and potassium. These castings serve as an excellent soil amendment, improving soil structure, fertility, and water-holding capacity.

Vermicomposting can be practiced at various scales, from small-scale home composting bins to large-scale agricultural systems, providing a sustainable way to manage organic waste while producing a valuable resource for plant growth.

6. Human-made Habitats:

Worms can also adapt to human-made habitats such as gardens, farmlands, and even urban environments. They can be found in vegetable patches, flower beds, potted plants, and even in green roofs, where they help break down organic matter and improve soil fertility. Worms can also thrive in sewer systems, feeding on organic waste and playing a role in wastewater treatment.

In gardens and agricultural settings, worms contribute to soil health and plant growth. Their burrowing activities improve soil structure, allowing better water penetration and root development. By creating tunnels, they promote aeration, water infiltration, and nutrient movement in the soil. Earthworms and other soil- dwelling worms also consume dead plant material and organic waste, breaking it down into simpler forms that can be readily absorbed by plants. This decomposition process releases nutrients, enhances soil fertility, and stimulates plant growth. Additionally, vermiculture systems can be set up in urban areas, utilizing worms to process organic waste and produce nutrient-rich vermicompost. These systems can be small-scale and suitable for urban environments, providing a sustainable solution for managing organic waste and producing a valuable resource for urban gardening.

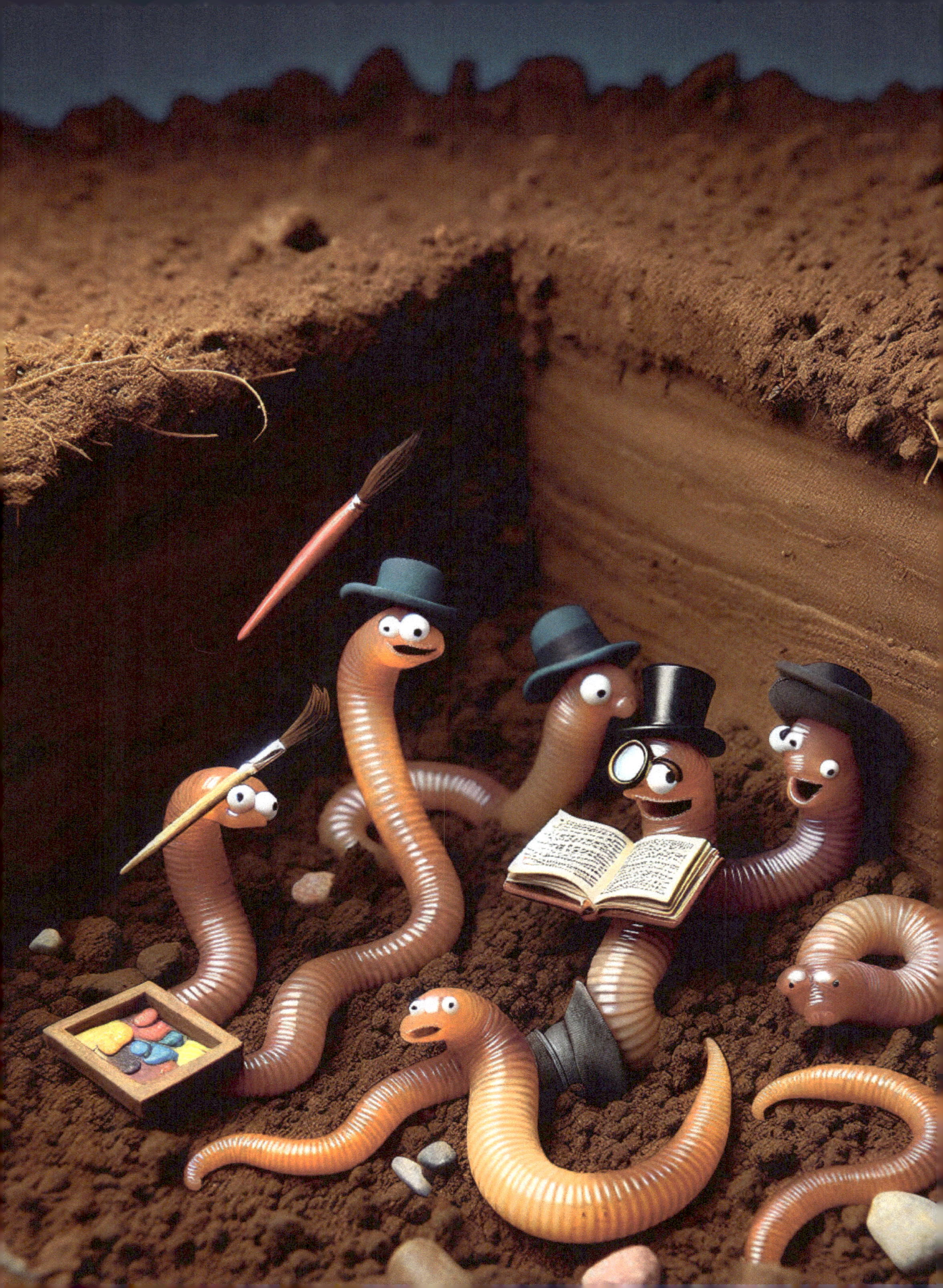

Worm Behavior

Worms may seem simple and unassuming creatures, but they exhibit fascinating behaviors that reveal their remarkable adaptability and survival strategies. In this chapter, we will delve into the intriguing world of worm behavior.

1. Movement and Navigation:

Worms are known for their distinctive way of getting around - using their muscles and bristles. They crawl and wriggle through the soil, feeling their way forward with the help of sensitive nerve endings on their skin. While they don't have eyes, worms possess photoreceptor cells that can detect light and help them navigate towards darker or moisture areas, which are more conducive to their survival. It is astonishing to think that these small creatures can orient themselves without traditional sensory organs.

2. Feeding Habits:

Worms are voracious eaters, consuming organic matter in the soil such as decaying leaves, dead plants, and microorganisms. They have a unique feeding behavior called geophagy, which involves ingesting small particles of soil along with their food. This behavior aids in the grinding and breakdown of food in their muscular gizzard, promoting efficient digestion. By consuming soil, worms also introduce beneficial microorganisms into their gut, helping them break down organic matter more effectively. Through their feeding habits, worms play a crucial role in nutrient cycling and soil fertility, contributing significantly to the health of ecosystems.

3. Burrowing and Tunnelling:

One of the most remarkable behaviors of worms is their ability to burrow deep into the ground and create intricate tunnels. By continuously moving and loosening the soil, worms improve its structure and aeration, promoting healthier soil ecosystems. The burrowing behavior also helps transport organic matter into deeper soil layers, facilitating nutrient cycling and decomposition. Moreover, the tunnels created by worms act as channels for water movement, preventing soil erosion and aiding in groundwater recharge. These tunnels also enable the exchange of gasses and nutrients between the surface and deep soil layers, enhancing overall soil health. This behavior of worms has a profoundly positive and long-lasting impact on the overall health and fertility of the soil.

4. Reproduction and Mating:

Worm reproduction is a fascinating process. Most commonly, worms are hermaphrodites, meaning they possess both male and female reproductive organs. During mating, worms exchange sperm packets, which are stored in special sacs. Although self-fertilization is possible, most worms engage in cross- fertilization, enhancing genetic diversity. The resultant cocoon, secreted by the clitellum, contains fertilized eggs that hatch into juvenile worms. This reproductive strategy ensures the continuation of the worm population and helps maintain genetic variability, which is vital for species adaptation and resilience. Interestingly, the timing of reproduction and cocoon hatching is influenced by environmental factors such as temperature and moisture levels, ensuring that the new generation of worms has the best chance of survival.

5. Response to Environmental Stimuli:

Despite their lack of a centralized brain, worms exhibit remarkable responses to various environmental stimuli. They are highly sensitive to changes in temperature, light, moisture, and even vibrations. Worms can quickly retract or move away from unfavorable conditions, displaying a rudimentary form of instinctual behavior.

Their ability to sense and respond to their surroundings is essential for their survival in ever-changing environments. Through their sensitivity to environmental cues, worms can seek out optimal conditions and avoid threats, ensuring their continued existence. For instance, when exposed to intense heat or dryness, worms can enter a state of dormancy known as aestivation, retreating into deeper layers of soil until more favorable conditions return.

6. Social Interactions:

While worms are often solitary creatures, they can also exhibit social behaviors. When resources are abundant, worms may aggregate in areas with a high concentration of organic matter. In these aggregations, worms exchange chemical signals, communicate through touch, and even engage in communal feeding activities. These social interactions play a role in population dynamics and resource distribution. Additionally, the exchange of chemical signals may serve as a form of communication, facilitating cooperative behaviors and potentially providing benefits to the collective group. This interconnectivity within worm communities not only enhances their resilience but also promotes the efficient utilization of resources, benefiting the entire ecosystem.

Understanding worm behavior provides valuable insight into the ecological functions they perform and their overall impact on soil health. Studying these behaviors not only enriches our knowledge of these fascinating creatures but also contributes to the development of sustainable agricultural practices and environmental conservation efforts.

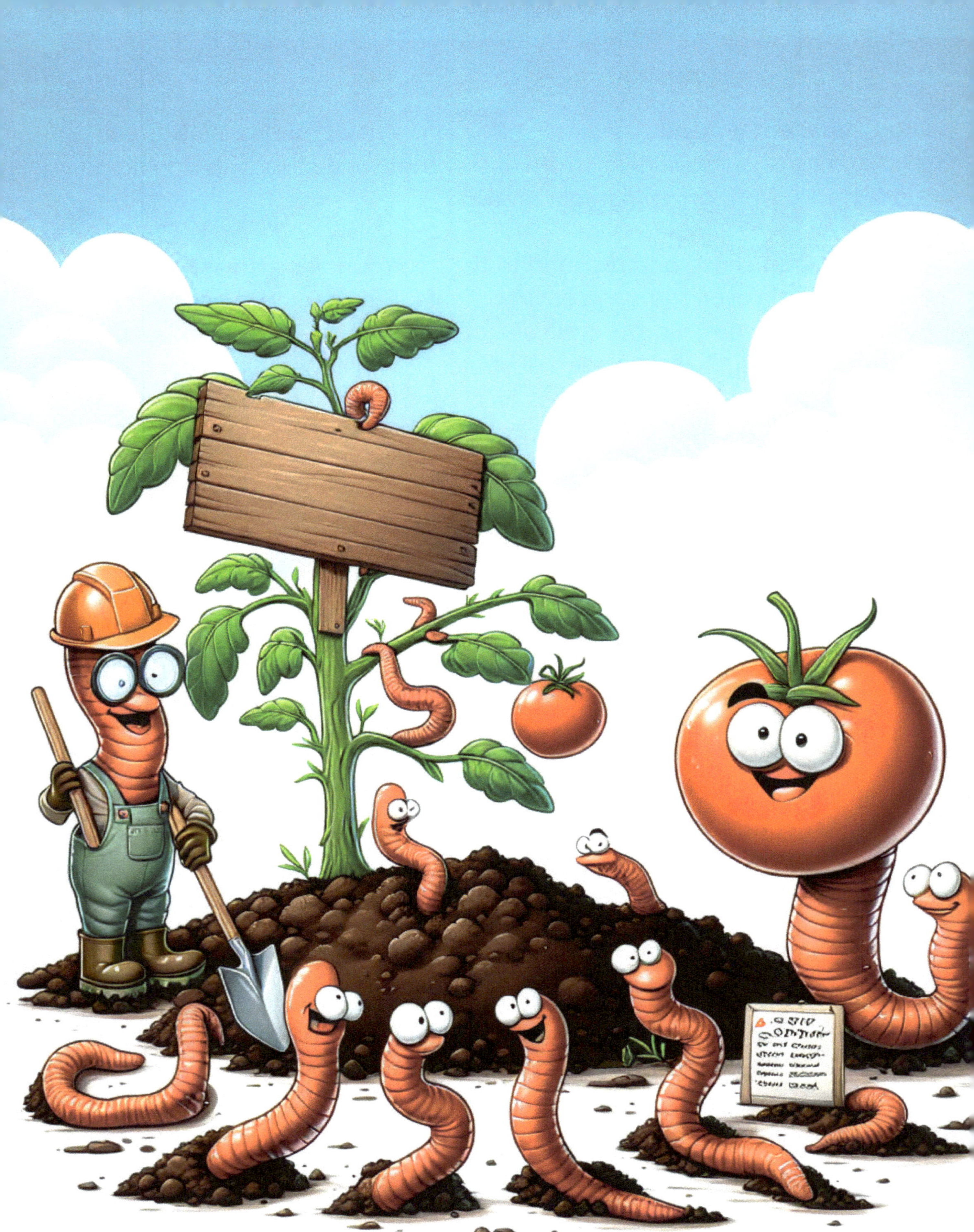

The Benefits of Worms

Worms are often overlooked and underestimated, but their contribution to our ecosystem is truly remarkable. These seemingly simple creatures have a profound impact on soil health, waste management, pollution control, ecosystem balance, and even scientific research. In this chapter, we will delve deeper into the incredible advantages of having worms in our environment.

One of the most significant benefits of worms lies in their role in soil health. As they digest organic matter, worms create vermicompost, a highly fertile substance that enriches the soil. This nutrient-rich compost not only enhances soil structure but also promotes healthy plant growth and increases crop productivity.

Vermicompost contains essential elements such as nitrogen, phosphorus, and potassium, along with beneficial microbes that assist in nutrient absorption by plants. Moreover, vermicompost enhances soil water-holding capacity, reducing the need for irrigation and preventing water runoff, thus conserving water resources.

The impact of worms on soil health goes beyond nutrient enrichment. Their burrowing activities help to improve soil aeration and drainage. As worms move through the soil, they create an intricate network of burrows and tunnels. These channels allow air and water to penetrate deeper into the ground, reaching the roots of plants and providing essential oxygen and moisture. As a result, the soil becomes more resilient and resistant to compaction, providing an ideal environment for root growth. Additionally, worm burrows help to alleviate problems caused by waterlogging, preventing plant diseases and root rot.

In addition to their contributions to soil health, worms are valuable in waste management. Vermiculture, the process of using worms to decompose organic waste, offers numerous environmental benefits. By feeding on kitchen scraps, garden waste, and other organic materials, worms break down these materials into nutrient-rich compost, diverting them from landfills and reducing greenhouse gas emissions. The use of vermicomposting systems in homes, schools, and communities not only helps to minimize waste but also empowers individuals to practice sustainable living and take active steps towards a circular economy.

Aside from their impact on waste management, worms possess a remarkable ability to aid in the detoxification of soil contaminated by pollutants. Certain species of worms, such as earthworms, can accumulate heavy metals in their tissues and reduce their concentration in the soil. Through their feeding and digestion process, worms break down organic pollutants, metabolizing and neutralizing harmful substances. This natural remediation process, known as bioremediation, has significant implications for cleaning up contaminated sites and restoring ecosystem health. Scientists are continuously exploring the potential of using worms to mitigate pollution and rehabilitate damaged environments.

Furthermore, worms play a vital role in maintaining ecosystem balance. As a food source for various animals, including birds, reptiles, amphibians, and small mammals, worms serve as an essential link in the food chain. Their high nutritional value ensures the survival and well-being of predator species, helping to maintain biodiversity and ecological stability. Additionally, worms attract insect-loving birds, contributing to natural pest control in gardens and agricultural fields. By supporting a diverse range of species, worms help to create resilient and vibrant ecosystems.

Beyond their ecological contributions, worms have also emerged as key players in scientific research and medical advancements. The nematode Caenorhabditis elegans, for example, has become a model organism in genetic and biological studies. With its transparent body and well-characterized genome, this tiny worm offers scientists valuable insights into human health and disease. Research involving C. elegans has shed light on various aspects of biology, including aging, neurodegenerative disorders, and cancer. The simplicity of the worm's anatomy and its quick reproductive cycle make it particularly useful for genetic experiments and drug testing. Moreover, C. elegans has played a significant role in deciphering fundamental genetic processes, such as RNA interference, that have revolutionized the field of molecular biology.

To fully grasp the magnitude of worms' contributions, one must recognize their multifaceted benefits. Their role as nature's plows, enriching soil with vermicompost, improving aeration and drainage, and preventing erosion, directly impacts agricultural productivity and sustainability. Additionally, their abilities in waste management, pollution control, and ecosystem balance have wide-ranging environmental implications. As our understanding of their significance deepens, scientists and ecologists are constantly uncovering new ways to leverage worms' remarkable capabilities to address pressing environmental challenges.

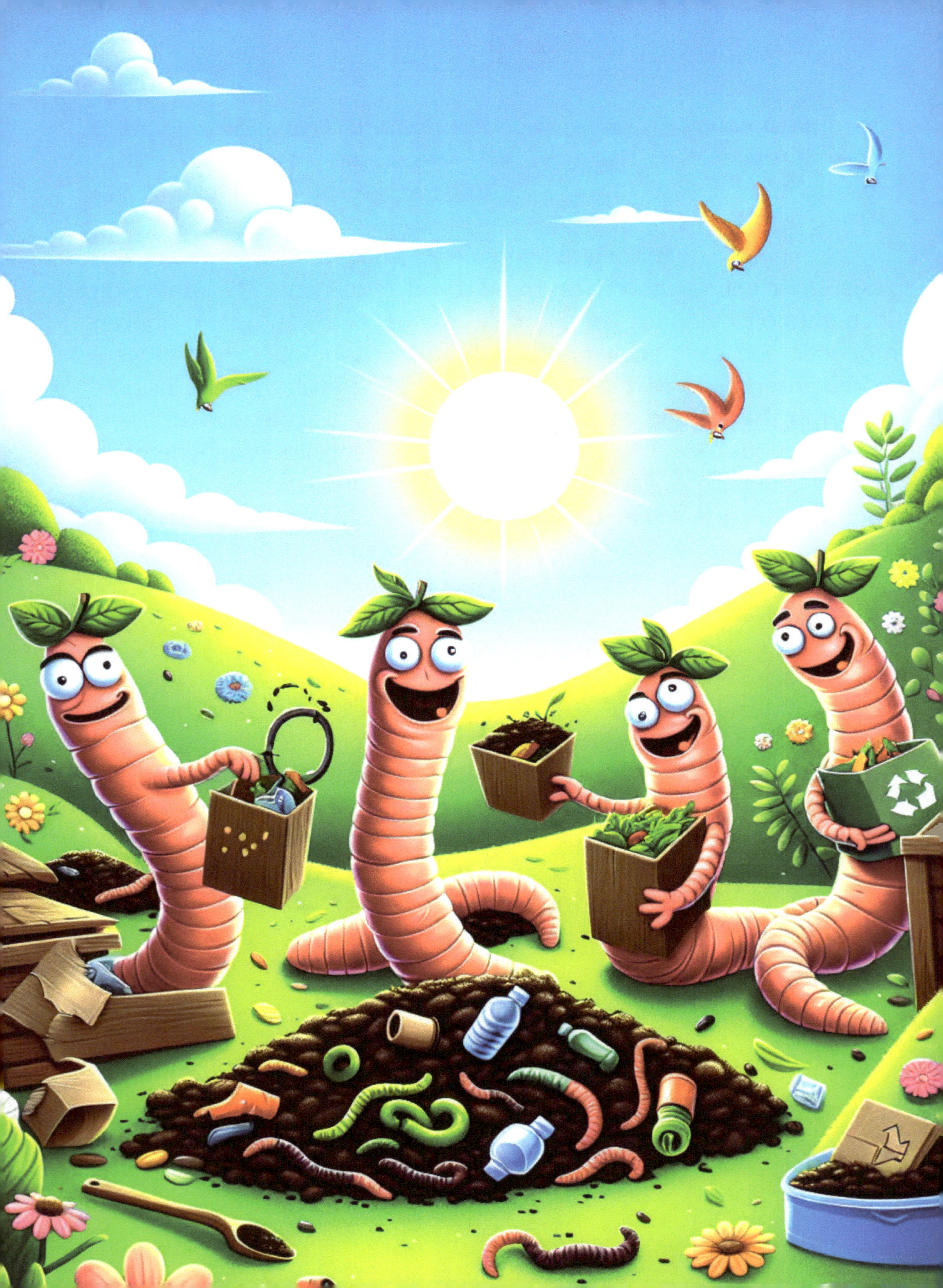

Worms and the Environment

Worms, the unsung heroes of the underground world, play a crucial role in maintaining a healthy environment. Through their activities, they contribute to various ecological processes that are essential for the functioning of ecosystems. Let's delve deeper into the ways in which worms interact with their environment and discover the astounding complexity of their impact.

1. Soil Improvement:

Worms are true architects of the soil, tirelessly burrowing through the earth and leaving behind a veritable network of channels. However, their impact goes far beyond simple tunneling. Earthworms have different species-specific behaviors that determine their burrowing patterns, such as vertical burrows, horizontal burrows, or mixing burrows. These behaviors influence the distribution of nutrients, water, and organic matter in the soil. For example, certain species create vertical burrows, which transport nutrients from the surface to deeper soil layers, while others create horizontal burrows that allow for the movement of water and nutrients laterally. By creating these tunnels, worms not only enhance soil structure, but also facilitate the movement of air, water, and nutrients throughout the soil profile. The passages they create act as conduits that allow roots to penetrate deeper into the ground, accessing vital resources. Through their relentless trudging, worms effectively mix different soil layers, ensuring a homogenized distribution of nutrients and creating an environment conducive to healthy plant growth.

2. Nutrient Cycling:

Worms are voracious consumers of organic matter, readily gobbling up dead leaves, decaying plant debris, and other organic waste. As they digest this organic material, their digestive systems break it down into simpler compounds, releasing nutrients in the process. Different species of worms have distinct preferences for various types of organic matter, resulting in different nutrient outputs. For instance, some species are particularly efficient at incorporating nitrogen-rich organic material, while others consume plant roots and contribute to the cycling of carbon. These nutrients, released through worm excrement or castings, are then transformed into highly concentrated capsules of fertility. Small in size but mighty in impact, worm castings are greatly appreciated by soil-dwelling organisms and plants alike. These casts are teeming with beneficial microorganisms that continue the decomposition process and further enhance nutrient availability. In this way, worms play a vital role in nutrient cycling, ensuring that valuable resources are efficiently recycled within the ecosystem.

3. Aeration and Drainage:

Picture the underground world as a bustling metropolis, with worms being the city planners, designing pathways for air and water circulation. As they move through the soil, worms create a vast network of tunnels, opening up previously compacted spaces. This process, called biopore formation, benefits soil aeration and drainage. The burrows created by worms act as ventilation shafts, allowing fresh air to penetrate deep into the soil profile. This enhanced aeration improves the activity of soil microorganisms, which play a crucial role in nutrient cycling and other soil processes. The increased availability of oxygen also supports the growth of aerobic organisms while suppressing anaerobic ones, leading to a more balanced soil microbial community. Moreover, the tunnel network created by worms serves as an efficient drainage system. During heavy rainfall, the intricate tunnels quickly absorb excess water, preventing water logging and facilitating water infiltration. By reducing the risk of runoff and erosion, worms contribute to maintaining healthy water cycles and preventing soil degradation.

4. Decomposition:

Worms are nature's efficient recyclers, adept at breaking down organic matter and accelerating the decomposition process. Their digestive systems contain a mix of bacteria, fungi, and other microorganisms that actively participate in the breakdown of organic material. These symbiotic relationships between worms and microorganisms not only aid digestion but also promote the breakdown of resistant compounds such as lignin. As worms consume this organic matter, they mechanically and chemically break it down, fragmenting it into smaller particles.

This fragmentation exposes more surface area to the activity of decomposer microbes, such as bacteria and fungi, unlocking the stored nutrients. Additionally, worm burrows provide a habitat for microorganisms, creating microsites with unique moisture, temperature, and nutrient conditions. These microsites further enhance decomposition rates and serve as hotspots for microbial activity. By accelerating decomposition, worms play a crucial role in maintaining the balance between organic inputs and nutrient outputs, ultimately sustaining the productivity of ecosystems.

5. Erosion Control:

In the battle against erosion, worms take on the role of soil guardians. By creating their intricate tunnels, they improve the stability of soil particles, preventing them from being easily dislodged by the forces of wind and water. The burrow walls create a network of interconnected pores that act like a sponge, absorbing rainfall and slowing down runoff. This sponge effect reduces the erosive impacts of heavy rainfall, preventing soil particles from being washed away. Moreover, their burrows enhance soil structure, promoting aggregation and creating a crumbly texture that further helps to prevent erosion. The stable soil structure, created and maintained by worms, acts as a protective barrier against the erosive forces of wind and water, decreasing the likelihood of soil loss and promoting soil conservation.

6. Biodiversity and Food Web:

Worms are not solitary creatures. They are an integral part of the vast and intricate web of life that exists beneath our feet. Worms provide a crucial source of food for a myriad of organisms, such as birds, small mammals, amphibians, and invertebrates. Their abundance and availability make them a key component of the trophic structure in ecosystems. In turn, the predators of worms also play essential roles within their respective habitats, contributing to the overall biodiversity and functioning of ecosystems. The interconnectedness of these species highlights the significance of worms as ecological connectors, linking primary producers with higher trophic levels. By supporting a diverse array of predators, worms contribute to the overall biodiversity of ecosystems. Their presence creates a delicate balance, ensuring the survival and abundance of other species, thereby maintaining the stability and resilience of the environment as a whole.

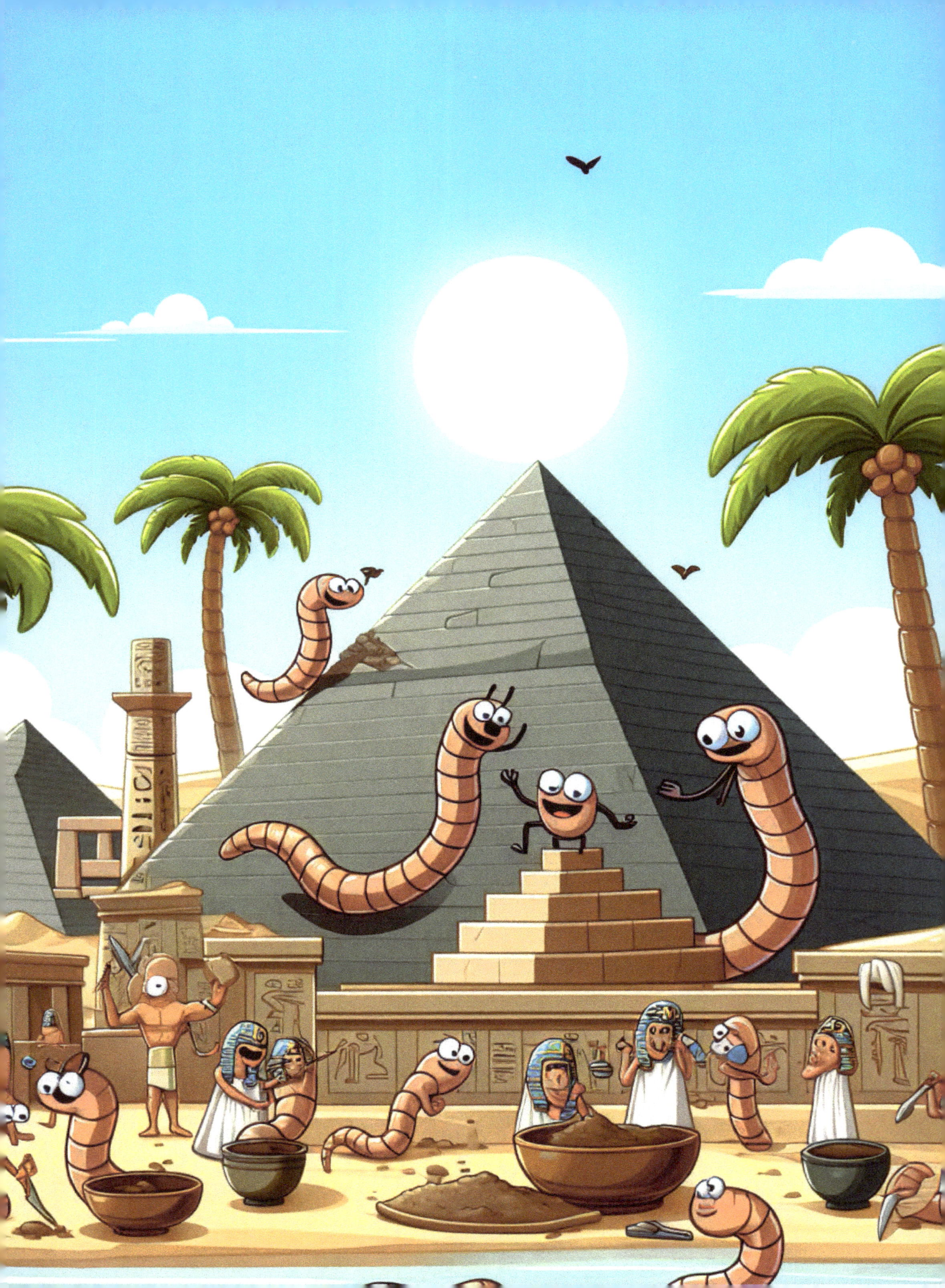

All About Worms

Worms and Human History

Throughout history, worms have played a significant role in shaping human civilization. From their role in agriculture and medicine to their impact on cultural beliefs and traditions, worms have left an indelible mark on our collective history. This chapter delves into the fascinating relationship between worms and human beings, exploring the ways in which these humble creatures have influenced our past.

1. Ancient Agriculture:

From ancient civilizations to contemporary farming practices, worms have been invaluable in improving soil fertility. The ancient Egyptians recognized the powerful effects of worm castings and used them to enrich their soils thousands of years ago. They understood that worms helped break down organic matter through their consumption and digestion processes, creating rich humus and releasing essential nutrients back into the soil. Similarly, ancient cultures in Mesopotamia and China discovered the benefits of vermiculture, utilizing worms in composting and soil conditioning. They observed that incorporating worms into agricultural practices enhanced soil structure, increased water retention, and facilitated nutrient uptake by plants. These ancient farming techniques laid the foundation for sustainable agricultural practices that continue to be embraced today.

The intricate relationship between worms and soil health is even more nuanced than previously understood. Recent studies have revealed that worm activity promotes the formation of stable aggregates of soil particles, creating a crumbly soil structure with improved porosity and water-holding capacity. These aggregates not only provide favorable conditions for plant root growth but also contribute to carbon sequestration, mitigating climate change by storing significant amounts of carbon in the soil. Furthermore, worms increase the activity and diversity of beneficial soil microorganisms, fostering a resilient and balanced soil ecosystem. These advancements in understanding the synergistic relationship between worms, soil, and plants have propelled sustainable agriculture to new heights, offering innovative approaches for regenerative farming practices and addressing global food security challenges.

2. Medicinal Uses:

Worms have long been used in traditional medicine across various cultures. Ancient healers believed in the healing properties of earthworms, using them to treat a variety of ailments. In China, worms were utilized in traditional medicine to alleviate joint pain, improve blood circulation, and boost the immune system.

Worms were also believed to have antimicrobial properties and were used in poultices to aid wound healing. The ancient Greeks and Romans also recognized the medicinal value of worms, using them to treat conditions such as intestinal disorders and even toothache. Their use in traditional medicine has continued to evolve, with ongoing research uncovering new therapeutic potentials of worms and their secretions.

Scientists have discovered a host of bioactive compounds in worms that possess antibacterial, antifungal, and anti-inflammatory properties. These compounds show promise in developing novel antibiotics to combat multidrug-resistant bacteria, as well as potential anti-cancer agents. Furthermore, a substance called "wormin" found in some earthworms has demonstrated immunomodulatory effects, suggesting its potential in treating autoimmune disorders and allergies. As researchers delve deeper into the molecular makeup of worms, exploring their complex chemical compositions, the potential for harnessing their therapeutic properties becomes increasingly exciting. The study of worm-based medicines, known as helminth therapy, is gaining traction in the medical community, as scientists investigate the potential use of worms to treat autoimmune diseases, such as inflammatory bowel disease and multiple sclerosis. This emerging field holds promise for future medical advancements, offering alternative treatment options in an era of increasing antibiotic resistance.

3. Cultural and Symbolic Significance:

Worms have found their way into folklore, myths, and religious beliefs throughout human history. In many indigenous cultures, worms are considered sacred creatures, symbolizing fertility and the cyclical nature of life. For example, the Aztecs believed that the earth gods transformed themselves into worms, signifying their connection to the land and the renewal of life. Similarly, in Aboriginal Dreamtime stories of Australia, worms are revered as creators and maintainers of the natural world. In ancient Norse mythology, the giant sea serpent Jormungandr, also known as the Midgard Serpent, was associated with chaos and destruction, illustrating the complex symbolism that worms held in different cultural contexts.

The symbolic significance of worms extends beyond their role in fertility and renewal; they have also served as metaphors for human existence and societal dynamics. The phrase "lowly worm" often appears in literature, representing humility and the underdog. In Charles Dickens' novel, "A Tale of Two Cities," Jerry Cruncher's side occupation of digging up graves for body-snatching is metaphorically akin to worms breaking down the dead. This metaphorical connection underscores the universal human fascination with worms and their connection to life, death, and renewal.

4. Scientific Discoveries:

Worms have played a crucial role in scientific breakthroughs, particularly in the fields of biology, ecology, and neuroscience. The eminent biologist Charles Darwin extensively studied worms and their impact on soil formation, recognizing their importance in the ecosystem. His groundbreaking research on worms, published in his book "The Formation of Vegetable Mold through the Action of Worms," not only advanced our understanding of soil ecology but also shed light on the processes of decomposition and nutrient cycling. Darwin's work on worms laid the foundation for vermiculture and contributed significantly to our understanding of evolutionary biology.

The significance of worms in scientific research has expanded beyond soil ecology and evolutionary biology. The roundworm Caenorhabditis elegans, a microscopic worm, has become a model organism for studying fundamental biological processes. Its transparent body and well-defined neural circuitry make it an ideal subject for investigating nervous system development, behavior, and aging.

Through the study of C. elegans, scientists have made remarkable discoveries, unraveling genetic pathways related to longevity, cellular differentiation, and even neuronal signaling. These findings have direct implications for human health and the understanding of neurodegenerative diseases such as Alzheimer's and Parkinson's. Additionally, worms have been crucial in studying the effects of space travel on living organisms. Experiments with worms on the International Space Station have provided insights into the impact of microgravity and cosmic radiation on muscle loss, aging, and tissue regeneration, potentially benefiting future space exploration and human health.

5. Environmental Indicator:

Worm populations can serve as indicators of environmental health. Various species of worms are highly sensitive to environmental changes, particularly in soil and aquatic ecosystems. Their presence or absence can provide valuable insights into soil quality, pollution levels, and overall ecosystem health. For instance, certain species of earthworms thrive in healthy soil, and their abundance can indicate soil fertility and beneficial microbial activity. Conversely, the absence of worms or dominance of certain pollution-tolerant species may indicate degraded or contaminated environments.

As environmental concerns deepen, the study of worms as bioindicators gains significance. Scientists are exploring the use of specific worm species to assess the quality of soil in urban environments and guide urban planning decisions. The presence of certain worm species can indicate the quality and functionality of ecosystem services within cities, such as nutrient cycling, soil structure maintenance, and water infiltration. Additionally, researchers are investigating the potential of aquatic worms as indicators of water pollution, as their sensitivity to contaminants can provide early warning signs of deteriorating water quality.

Worms have quietly influenced human history in profound ways, going beyond their role in agriculture and medicine. Whether through their contribution to sustainable farming practices, traditional healing methods, cultural symbolism, scientific research, or environmental monitoring, these unassuming creatures have left an indelible mark on our collective human experience. From ancient civilizations to modern society, worms have played a vital role in shaping our understanding of the natural world and our place within it.

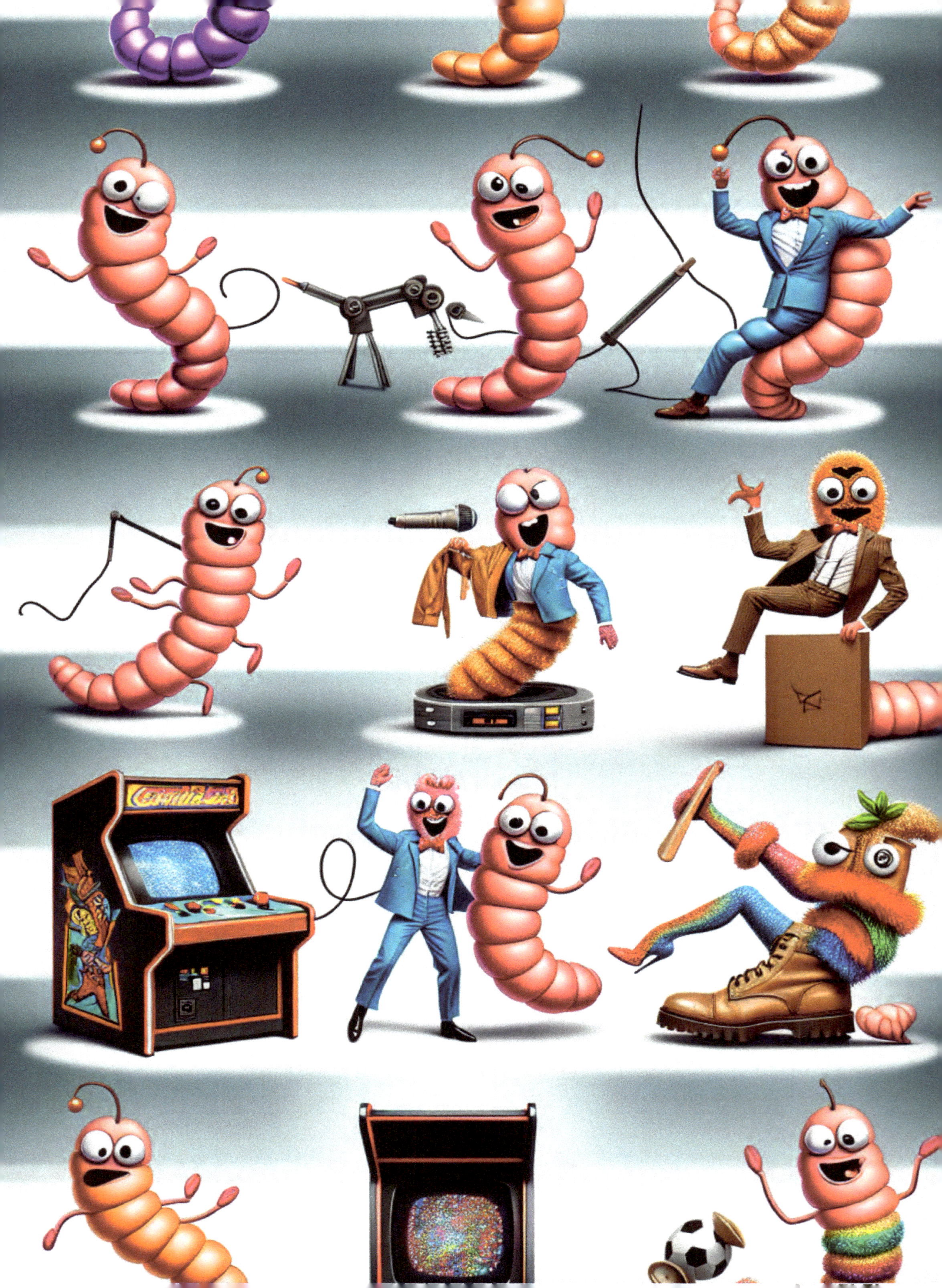

Worms in Pop Culture

Worms, despite being humble creatures that typically reside underground, have found their way into various forms of popular culture. From books to cartoons, movies, and even video games, worms have been portrayed in different and often humorous ways. This chapter explores the goofy side of worms in pop culture.

One of the most iconic representations of worms in popular culture is the character "Worm" from the animated television series "SpongeBob SquarePants." Worm is a friendly, yet somewhat dimwitted, character with a high-pitched voice. He is often seen getting into comical situations and offering amusing lines that endear him to viewers of all ages. Worm's goofy and lovable personality has made him a fan favorite and a memorable addition to the show.

However, SpongeBob SquarePants is not the only animated series that has embraced the goofiness of worms. Another notable mention is the cartoon series "Wormy" from the show "The Fairly OddParents." In this episode, Timmy Turner turns into a worm and hilarity ensues. The exaggerated worm features, like big googly eyes and a permanent toothy grin, create a comical contrast to the otherwise ordinary world. This episode not only highlights the humor associated with worms but also explores themes of empathy and acceptance. By showcasing the goofiness of worms in this heartfelt manner, "Wormy" resonates with viewers and creates a lasting impact.

The 1999 film "Earthworm Jim" also contributed to the representation of worms in pop culture. This animated adventure introduced Jim, a comedic superhero worm with a powerful robotic suit. Jim's journey to save Princess What's-Her-Name from various antagonists showcases the absurdity of the situation, leading to humorous encounters and witty dialogue. By blending action, humor, and a unique concept, "Earthworm Jim" expanded the goofy representation of worms in pop culture, appealing to a broader audience.

In the literary world, worms have also found their way into goofy storylines. For example, in the children's book "Diary of a Worm" by Doreen Cronin, readers are taken on hilarious adventures through the eyes of a young worm. Through humorous diary entries, the book delves into the everyday life of a worm, complete with funny anecdotes about his family, friends, and experiences in the underground world. This lighthearted and whimsical approach not only highlights the humorous side of worms but also educates children about the wonders of nature in an entertaining way.

Moreover, worms have made appearances in video games that embrace a playful and comedic tone. "Worms," a popular turn-based strategy game released in 1995, depicts worms as quirky soldiers armed with an arsenal of comical weapons.

Players command their team of worms to destroy opponents' teams in absurd scenarios, complete with outlandish explosions, hilarious sound effects, and humorous dialogue. The game's playful depiction of worms adds an element of goofy fun, making it a favorite among gamers of all ages.

Not only have worms permeated children's literature and video games, but they have also left their mark on adult-oriented humor. In the adult animated series "Rick and Morty," worms make an appearance in the episode titled "Lawnmower Dog." In this episode, the main characters venture into the dreams of their family dog, Snowball, who gains intelligence and starts a revolution of sentient dogs. In one dream sequence, Snowball leads an army of dogs against the tyranny of humans, with a giant worm-like creature acting as his advisor. This unconventional portrayal of worms within a complex and engaging storyline adds an extra layer of satire and absurdity, further showcasing the endless comedic potential of worms in pop culture.

In the realm of movies, worms have been featured in humorous and light-hearted films that showcase their silly and comedic potential. For instance, the movie "Men in Black" introduces a charming character known as "Frank the Pug." Despite his name, Frank is actually an extraterrestrial who takes the form of a small, talking pug dog. One of his memorable aspects is the revelation that his head is actually a disguise controlled by a tiny worm-like creature inside. This quirky depiction of worms as part of a comedic alien character adds a touch of wit and amusement to the flm.

Beyond these specific examples, worms have permeated pop culture through various forms of media, embracing their goofy side. From beloved characters in animated series like "SpongeBob SquarePants," "The Fairly OddParents," and "Rick and Morty" to their playful appearances in children's books, video games, and movies, worms have shown that they can bring humor and amusement to audiences of all ages. These portrayals offer a refreshing perspective on worms, reminding us that even the simplest creatures can elicit laughter and joy in our lives.

The inclusion of worms in pop culture, particularly in goofy ways, reflects society's fascination with finding humor and amusement in unexpected places. By portraying worms in a lighthearted and comical manner, these depictions help to break the stereotype of worms as solely slimy and uninteresting creatures. Instead, they showcase the whimsical side of worms, highlighting their potential for laughter and entertainment.

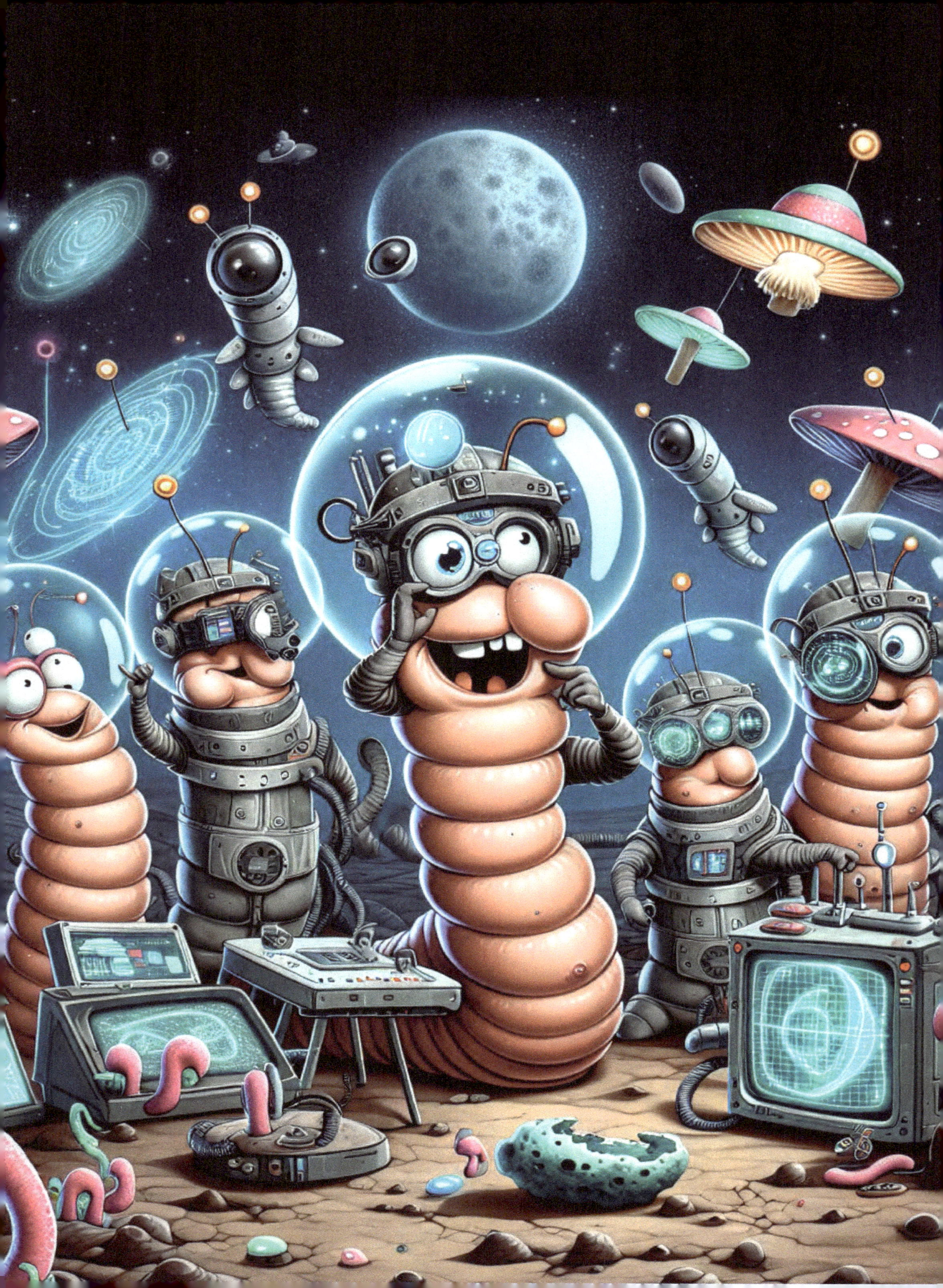

All About Worms

Worms in Science Fiction

Worms have long captivated the imagination of writers, particularly when it comes to the realm of science fiction. Through vivid storytelling and imaginative concepts, worms have been depicted in various futuristic scenarios, often taking on roles beyond their earthly existence. In this chapter, we will explore the intriguing presence of worms in science fiction literature and how they have been portrayed in this genre.

One prominent example of worms in science fiction is Frank Herbert's masterpiece, "Dune." Published in 1965, this epic novel introduced readers to the giant sandworms of the desert planet Arrakis. These colossal creatures, capable of growing up to several hundred meters in length, played a crucial role in the intricate ecosystem depicted in the story. They not only shaped the physical environment of the planet with their burrowing, but also became revered creatures by the indigenous Fremen, who saw them as deities. The sandworms' interactions with the human characters and their ability to produce the highly coveted spice known as melange created a rich and imaginative narrative. Herbert's creation of the sandworms added a unique and thought-provoking element to the science fiction genre, exploring themes of ecology, religion, and the symbiotic relationship between humankind and the environment.

Worms have also found their way into science fiction as alien species. H.G. Wells, known as the father of science fiction, incorporated worms into his imaginative universe. In his novel, "The War of the Worlds," Wells describes gigantic tentacled creatures called tripods that were operated by mollusk-like aliens from Mars.

These extraterrestrial beings used their advanced technology and worms as weapons of destruction, showcasing the fusion of science and imagination in the genre. Wells' portrayal of worms in science fiction helped pave the way for future writers to explore the possibilities of these creatures as both allies and adversaries to humanity, raising questions about the boundaries of knowledge and the potential threats posed by extraterrestrial life forms.

Another notable mention is Robert A. Heinlein's classic novel "Starship Troopers." In this military science fiction tale, Heinlein introduced the concept of "skinnies," a species resembling Earth's worms. These skinnies, inhabiting the planet Skinn, played a significant role within the intergalactic conflict, serving as a means of dissecting humanity's understanding of alien life forms. By incorporating worms into his story, Heinlein emphasized the diversity and complexity of extraterrestrial life, further expanding the boundaries of science fiction. He challenged readers to consider the intricacies of communication, perception, and the potential for understanding across species boundaries.

Furthermore, worms have also been depicted as intelligent beings capable of advanced communication and intellect. This can be seen in Vernor Vinge's "A Fire Upon the Deep," where he introduces the Tines, a multi-bodied race resembling dogs, but with an intricate communication system facilitated by implanted worm- like structures. The Tines' communication relies on the intricate interplay of different individuals forming a larger collective mind. Vinge's portrayal of worms as a means of interstellar communication portrays them as an intriguing and unique life form, challenging readers to question traditional notions of intelligence, consciousness, and the possibilities of communication in diverse forms.

In addition to these examples, worms have been explored in various other science fiction works. In Philip K. Dick's "Do Androids Dream of Electric Sheep?", the book that inspired the film "Blade Runner," genetically engineered worms play a crucial role in the dystopian world he created. These worms, known as "electric animals," act as status symbols for characters who cannot afford real animals due to their scarcity. Dick's incorporation of worms into his futuristic landscape highlights themes of artificiality, the blurred lines between reality and simulation, and the human desire for connection and authenticity.

In the award-winning novella "Binti " by Nnedi Okorafor, alien species known as the Meduse are humanoid in shape but possess transformative characteristics. When threatened, these beings can change their outer structure, taking on worm-like features. Okorafor's portrayal of these Meduse worms serves as a powerful symbol of adaptability and resilience, while exploring themes of identity, understanding, and reconciliation between different cultures.

Furthermore, the presence of worms in science fiction can also be found beyond creatures and aliens. In the classic time travel novel "Doomsday Book" by Connie Willis, a plague-ridden society is disrupted further when a character accidentally gets sent back in time to the Middle Ages. As the protagonist navigates the challenges of this new era, she finds worms to be integral to daily life, both as a source of nourishment and as indicators of disease. Through this narrative device, Willis examines the interconnectedness of all living beings and the universal struggles faced by humanity throughout history.

Beyond individual works, the recurring presence of worms in science fiction hints at the deep-rooted fascination humans have with these creatures. Their association with environmental change, transformation, and adaptability appeals to our longing for a better understanding of our own world and our place in the vast cosmos. Whether serving as symbols of otherworldly power, conduits for communication, or agents of transformation, worms in science fiction continue to captivate readers and spark discussions about our existence, our relationship with the natural world, and the unknown realm of possibilities.

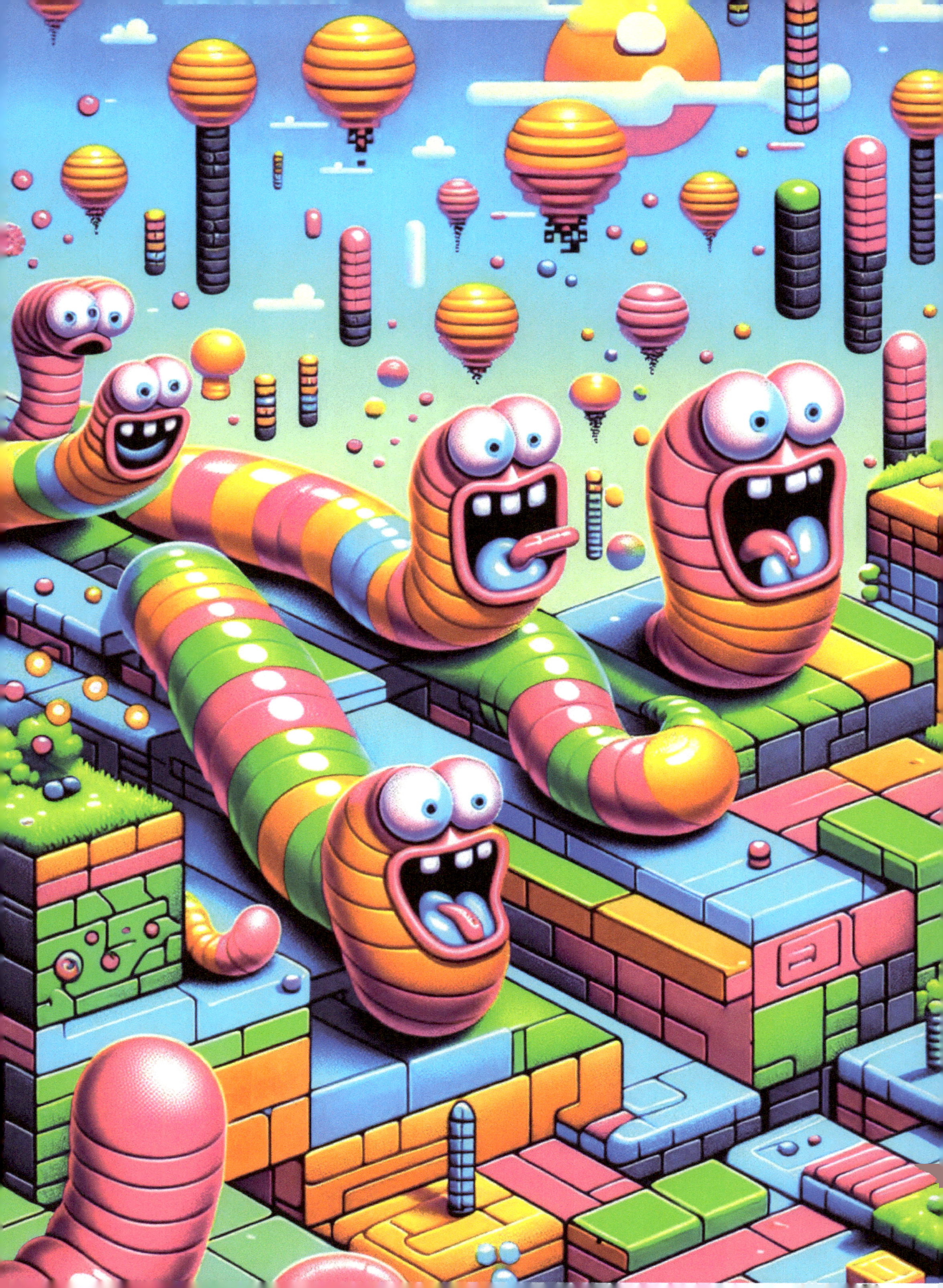

Worms in Digital Realms

In this digital age, technology has permeated every aspect of our lives. We find ourselves interconnected through the vast expanse of the internet, exploring a realm that knows no physical boundaries. It is within this digital realm that worms, once limited to the soil, have found a new existence. Today, we delve into the fascinating world of worms in digital realms.

The Origin of Digital Worms

Digital worms, much like their organic counterparts, have their own unique origins. In the realm of computer science, they are known as a type of malicious software, or malware, that can self-replicate and spread across computer networks. The concept of digital worms emerged in the 1980s when Robert Tappan Morris, a graduate student at Cornell University, inadvertently created the first documented computer worm, known as the Morris Worm. This incident highlighted the potential for self-replicating programs to cause widespread damage.

Propagation and Behavior

Unlike the physical world, digital worms do not require soil or physical contact to propagate. They rely on the interconnectedness of digital networks to spread, exploiting vulnerabilities in operating systems and applications. These vulnerabilities can be as simple as outdated software or as complex as zero-day exploits, which are unknown vulnerabilities.

Once a host is infected, the worm can then spread to other devices within the network, creating a chain of infection. It can use various methods to propagate, such as spreading through email attachments, network shares, or even exploiting security flaws in network protocols. Some worms can also exploit human behavior, tricking users into clicking on malicious links or downloading infected files.

Digital worms, much like their organic counterparts, possess unique behaviors. They can exhibit stealthy features, evading detection by antivirus software, firewalls, and other security mechanisms. Some worms possess mechanisms to disable or evade removal tools, making them highly resilient. Advanced worms can also have polymorphic or metamorphic characteristics, changing their structure or appearance to avoid detection.

The Impact of Digital Worms

The impact of digital worms is far-reaching, affecting not only individuals but also the global economy. Worms can disrupt critical infrastructure, such as power grids, transportation systems, and communication networks. For instance, the Stuxnet worm, discovered in 2010, specifically targeted industrial control systems, causing physical damage to Iran's nuclear facilities. This incident showcased the potential for cyber attacks to have real-world consequences.

In addition to infrastructure disruption, worms can compromise personal information, leading to identity theft and financial loss. They can steal sensitive data, such as credit card details, social security numbers, or login credentials, and use it for malicious purposes. Moreover, worms can jeopardize national security by infiltrating government networks and stealing classified information. The consequences of such breaches can be severe, affecting geo-political stability and citizen trust.

Prevention and Mitigation

Given the potential havoc digital worms can wreak, it is crucial to implement preventive measures and mitigation strategies to protect ourselves and our digital ecosystems. The following strategies can help minimize the risk of infection:

1. Regular Software Updates: Keeping operating systems, applications, and security software up to date is essential to patch vulnerabilities that may be exploited by worms. Software developers often release updates to fx vulnerabilities discovered over time, making regular updates crucial in maintaining a secure digital environment.

2. Strong Passwords and Secure Authentication: Using strong, unique passwords and enabling multi-factor authentication can significantly enhance security. Weak passwords are easy targets for brute-force attacks, allowing worms to infiltrate systems easily. Multi-factor authentication adds an extra layer of protection by requiring additional verification steps, making it harder for worms to compromise accounts.

3. Network Segmentation: Dividing computer networks into smaller segments or zones with limited access helps contain the spread of worms. If a worm infects one segment, it will be more difficult for it to traverse to other areas, reducing the potential damage.

4. Education and Awareness: Organizations and individuals must prioritize cybersecurity education and awareness programs. By educating individuals on the importance of safe online practices, such as avoiding suspicious links and email attachments, recognizing phishing attempts, and being cautious with downloads, we can collectively reduce vulnerability to digital worms.

5. Intrusion Detection and Prevention Systems: Implementing robust intrusion detection and prevention systems can enhance network security by actively monitoring network traffic for malicious activity. These systems can identify and respond to potential worm infections, blocking and isolating infected hosts.

6. Incident Response and Recovery Plans: Having well-defined incident response and recovery plans can mitigate the impact of worm infections. These plans outline steps to detect, contain, eradicate, and recover from an attack efficiently, minimizing damage and reducing downtime.

As we venture further into the realms of digital connectivity, the presence of digital worms reminds us of the need for vigilance and proactive cybersecurity measures. Understanding their origins, propagation, behaviors, and impact helps us navigate the digital world with greater confidence and resilience. By adopting preventive measures, regularly updating software, using strong authentication methods, implementing network segmentation, prioritizing cybersecurity education, and investing in intrusion detection and prevention systems, we can safeguard our digital realms against the intrusion of these formidable digital creatures.

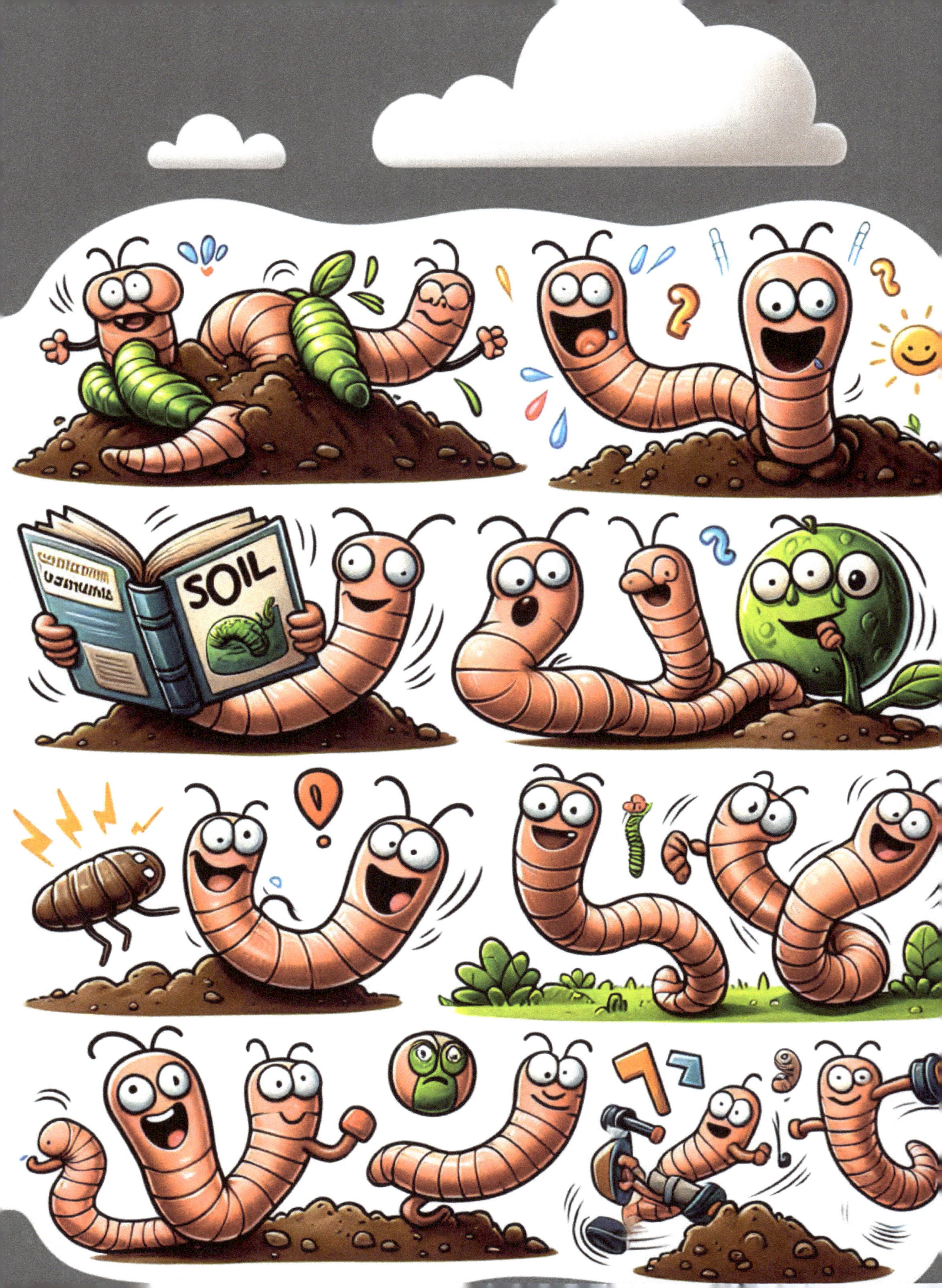
SOIL

Fun Facts about Worms

Worms may seem like simple creatures, but they are actually quite fascinating. Here are some extended fun facts about worms that will take you even deeper into their intriguing world:

1. Worms have been around for a long time. Fossils of worms dating back over 500 million years have been found, making them one of the oldest creatures on Earth. These resilient creatures have survived mass extinctions and environmental changes throughout history, adapting to various habitats and climates.

2. While we commonly associate worms with the ground, there are also species of worms that live in water, such as marine worms and freshwater worms. In marine environments, worms play vital roles in ecosystems. For example, tube-dwelling worms help stabilize sediments, preventing erosion and providing homes for other organisms. In freshwater ecosystems, worms serve as an integral part of the food chain, serving as a food source for various fish, birds, and amphibians.

3. Did you know that worms have both male and female reproductive organs? This unique characteristic means that they are hermaphrodites and can exchange sperm with another worm during mating. However, worms still require a partner to reproduce successfully, as self-fertilization rarely occurs in these creatures. During mating, worms align their bodies, exchanging sperm through specialized mating pores

called genital openings. This process ensures genetic diversity within their populations.

4. Worms are incredibly beneficial for soil health. As they burrow through the ground, they create tunnels that allow air and water to reach plant roots. The tunnels also promote the growth of microorganisms in the soil, enhancing its fertility. Additionally, their waste, called castings, are rich in nutrients that plants need to grow. These castings contain a higher concentration of nitrogen, phosphorus, and potassium compared to the surrounding soil, making worm castings a valuable natural fertilizer that farmers and gardeners use to improve soil quality and increase crop yields.

5. If you ever cut a worm in half, contrary to popular belief, it won't magically regenerate into two worms. While some worms, like the common earthworm, have the ability to regenerate their tails if they are damaged, the head-end cannot grow into a new worm. Despite this, worms do have remarkable regenerative capabilities. If a worm loses a segment containing reproductive organs, it can regenerate them, ensuring its ability to reproduce.

6. Worms don't have lungs; instead, they respire through their skin, a process called cutaneous respiration. Oxygen from the air diffuses into thin-walled blood vessels near the skin's surface and then passes into the circulatory system. Carbon dioxide, a byproduct of respiration, also diffuses out through the skin. This unique adaptation allows worms to respire efficiently while living underground, where oxygen levels may be lower compared to the atmosphere above.

7. Earthworms are true diggers. In fact, they can ingest soil that weighs up to their own weight in just one day! They consume organic matter in the soil, digesting it using the help of specialized enzymes produced

by cells in their intestinal walls. Nutrients are then absorbed through the intestine, and the remaining waste is eliminated as castings. This continuous process of feeding and digestion helps break down organic matter, allowing soil microorganisms to further decompose it, resulting in enhanced soil fertility and structure.

8. Some worms are social creatures. Take the fascinating glowworm, for example. Although not an actual worm, the larval stage of certain insects within the family Lampyridae surely deserves mention. These luminescent larvae use bioluminescent chemicals to create a glow that attracts prey, usually small insects. They emit a soft green light from specialized light-emitting organs to lure their unsuspecting victims. The glowworm's bioluminescence is an incredibly efficient hunting mechanism, allowing it to attract prey while remaining hidden from potential predators.

9. Worms are important decomposers. They play a crucial role in breaking down dead plant material, such as leaves and twigs, accelerating the decaying process. Through their feeding activities, worms fragment organic matter into smaller particles, providing an accessible food source for bacteria, fungi, and other decomposers. This organic matter breakdown not only helps recycle nutrients but also prevents the environment from becoming overwhelmed by dead organic matter, promoting ecosystem health and balance.

10. Lastly, worms have an incredible sense of touch. Their entire body is covered in sensitive nerve endings, allowing them to feel vibrations and changes in their environment. This tactile sensitivity helps them navigate through the soil, detect the presence of potential mates, and avoid threats such as predators or harsh conditions. Through their sensitive skin, worms can perceive variations in temperature, moisture levels, and

soil composition, enabling them to fnd optimal conditions for survival and reproduction.

These extended fun facts about worms showcase just a fraction of their vast and intricate world. From their ancient lineage to their diverse habitats, peculiar reproductive strategies, and indispensable roles in ecosystems, worms continue to captivate us with their remarkable adaptations and contributions to the natural world. They truly are tiny heroes, often underappreciated, but essential for the health and balance of our planet's diverse ecosystems.

All About Worms

Glossary

1. **Anecic:** A type of earthworm that makes vertical burrows deep in the soil.

2. **Architectural Artists:** Worms that build special underground structures.

3. **Burrowers:** Worms that create tunnels in the soil.

4. **Circulatory System:** The system in worms that moves nutrients and oxygen.

5. **Composters:** Worms that turn dead plants into nutritious soil.

6. **Digestive System:** A worm's system for eating and processing food.

7. **Earth King:** A large, wise earthworm that rules the worm kingdom.

8. **Endogeic:** Earthworms that burrow horizontally in the soil.

9. **Epigeic:** Earthworms that live on the soil surface and eat leaf litter.

10. **Freshwater Habitats:** Places in rivers or lakes where worms live.

11. **Gatherers:** Worms that collect and store food.

12. **Hemolymph:** Fluid in worms for carrying food and oxygen.

13. **Human-made Habitats:** Areas like gardens where worms aid the soil.

14. **Leaf Litter:** Dead leaves where some worms live and eat.

15. **Marine Habitats:** Ocean areas where certain worms live.

16. **Metameres:** Sections of a worm's body.

17. **Nematoda:** A group of round, long worms.

18. **Nervous System:** Helps worms sense and respond to their environment.

19. **Platyhelminthes:** Flat worms, some living in water or as parasites.

20. **Polychaetes:** Sea worms with many bristles.

21. **Prostomium:** The front part of a worm used for sensing and eating.

22. **Recyclers/Detritivores:** Worms that eat dead plants and animals.

23. **Reproductive System:** How worms reproduce with both male and female parts.

24. **Respiratory System:** How worms breathe through their skin.

25. **Setae:** Tiny bristles on a worm for movement and sensing.

26. **Soil Habitats:** Various types of soil where worms can live.

27. **Subterranean Universe:** The underground world of worms.

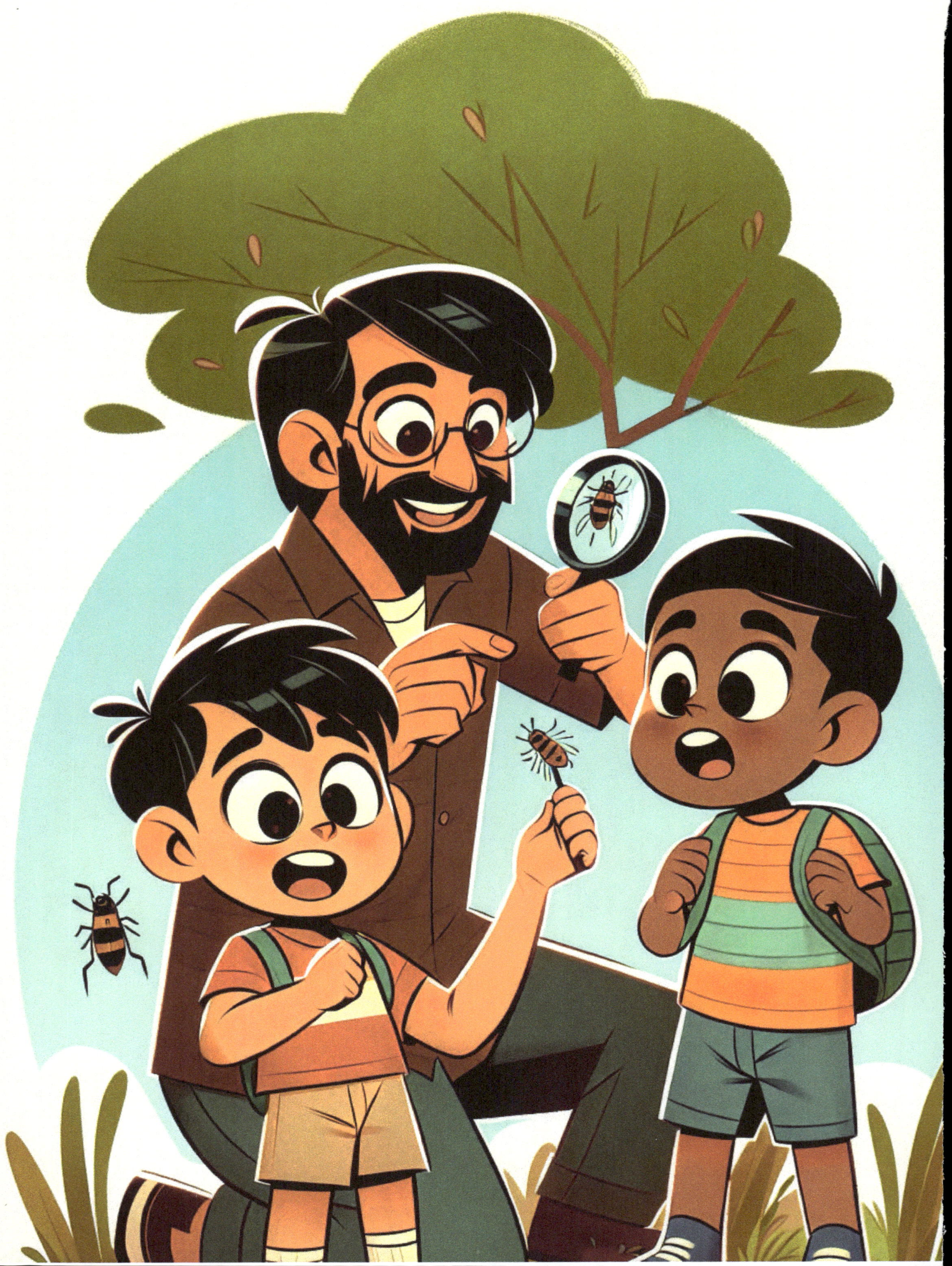

All About Worms

The Bug Collective, founded by a dad and his two sons, is an inspiring family venture rooted in a shared passion for the fascinating world of insects.

Born from a simple backyard exploration, their interest in bugs blossomed into a creative endeavor. They aim to craft engaging and informative books about the entomological wonders they discover.

Through their work, they seek to ignite curiosity and foster a deeper appreciation for the intricate lives of bugs in readers young and old. The Bug Collective is more than a publishing venture; it's a celebration of nature's tiny marvels, brought to you by a family that finds joy in every creepy crawler and fluttering wing.